EARTH HEROES

Champions
of the Wilderness

By Bruce and Carol L. Malnor
Illustrations by Anisa Claire Hovemann

DAWN Publications

DEDICATIONS

We hope you find inspiration in these pages and joy in wild places. — BRM and CLM

To my parents, Glenn and Muffy, for sharing their deep love of nature with me and the world. — ACH

Special thanks to the following organizations and individuals for their contributions: The Thoreau Institute at Walden Woods, www.walden.org/Institute; Aaron Yates; Martin Schwalbaum, www.4peaks. com; University of the Pacific Library, library.uop.edu; The Aldo Leopold Foundation, www.aldoleopold.org; The Wisconsin Historical Society, www.wisconsinhistory.org; The Murie Center Archives, www.muriecenter.org; Findhorn Foundation, www.findhorn.org; International Tree Foundation, www.internationaltreefoundation.org; Dana Stahlman, EAS Master Beekeeper, host of www.gobeekeeping.com; David Suzuki and the David Suzuki Foundation, www. davidsuzuki.org; Canadian Broadcasting Corporation, www.cbc.ca; The Green Belt Movement, www.greenbeltmovement. org; Marlborough Productions, www.takingrootfilm.com.

Copyright © 2009 Bruce and Carol Malnor
Illustration copyright © 2009 Anisa Claire Hovemann

All rights reserved.

Library of Congress Cataloging-in-Publication Data

Malnor, Bruce.
  Earth heroes : champions of the wilderness / by Bruce and Carol Malnor ; illustrated by Anisa Claire Hovemann.
-- 1st ed.
    p. cm.
  Summary: "The youth, careers and lasting contributions of some of the world's greatest naturalists and environmentalists are featured in this series of books on champions of the wilderness, oceans, and wildlife, this volume focused on wilderness" – Provided by the publisher.
  Includes bibliographical references and index.
  ISBN 978-1-58469-116-7 (pbk.)
  1. Environmentalists--Biography--Juvenile literature. I. Malnor, Carol. II. Hovemann, Anisa Claire, ill. III. Title.
  GE55.M35 2009
  333.72092'2--dc22
  [B]   2008053670

Printed in U.S.A.

10 9 8 7 6 5 4 3 2

First Edition

Book design and computer production by
Patty Arnold, *Menagerie Design and Publishing.*

DAWN PUBLICATIONS
12402 Bitney Springs Road
Nevada City, CA 95959
530-274-7775
nature@dawnpub.com

TABLE OF CONTENTS

Introduction: Who's a Hero? What's a Wilderness?   4

Henry David Thoreau: *Sage of Walden*   6
1817-1862

John Muir: *Speaker for the Wilderness*   22
1838-1914

Theodore Roosevelt: *The Conservation President*   38
1858-1919

Aldo Leopold: *Father of Forest Wilderness Conservation*   54
1887-1948

Richard St. Barbe Baker: *Man of the Trees*   70
1889 –1982

Margaret Murie: *Grandmother of the Conservation Movement*   86
1902–2003

David Suzuki: *Environmental Activist*   104
1936 — present

Wangari Maathai: *Tree Mother of Africa*   120
1940 — present

Conclusion: Become a Hero!   136

About the Authors and Illustrator   139

Notes and Credits   140

Index   142

Who's a Hero? What's a Wilderness?

Who do you think of when you think of a hero? Is it someone who accomplished a great feat? Or someone whose example inspired others? It might be someone who acted bravely to do what they felt was right even when others thought they were wrong. This book introduces you to eight people who did all of these things to preserve and protect the environment. They are truly "Earth Heroes."

These heroes are also called "Champions of the Wilderness" because they have supported and protected wild places around the world. What is wilderness? Wilderness is a wild place in nature where animals and plants live undisturbed. People may go there, but only to retreat from civilization and reconnect with the Earth. These champions found wilderness in spectacular places like Yosemite Valley. They also found it in smaller places close to home like the woods around Walden Pond.

Some of the heroes helped preserve huge areas of wilderness before it was lost to human development. Thanks to them, many mountains, glaciers, rivers, and meadows have remained wild and free. We can experience their untamed beauty today. Other heroes worked to restore nature's balance after a wilderness area was destroyed. Their actions show us that we can help the Earth's wild places to heal.

There have been many heroes of the wilderness throughout history. Many more are living today. From all of the possible people to choose from, the heroes included in this book represent some of the greatest wilderness environmentalists of all time—men and women from the past as well as the present, from the U.S. as well as other countries. Other books in this series feature heroes who focused their attention on the oceans, *Earth Heroes: Champions of the Oceans*, and wildlife, *Earth Heroes: Champions of Wildlife*.

A person's entire life can't be captured in just a few pages. This book gives you a "snapshot" of these heroes, especially on the childhood events and early experiences that shaped their lives. You'll discover who influenced them to care about the environment. You'll also find out how their actions influenced others. To get a quick summary of a hero, turn to the "Fast Facts" and "Timeline" at the end of each biography.

In historical writing, people are usually referred to by their last names. Because this book takes a very personal look at these champions, their first names are used. Each biography also includes several direct quotations—the actual words spoken or written by the person. After reading their stories, you'll feel like they're your friends.

Every person is unique, yet several aspects of these champions' lives are similar:

They had nature experiences when they were children.
Teddy Roosevelt discovered a seal skull when he was seven and used it to start his own nature museum. As a teenager, Mardy Murie took a dogsled ride through Alaska's wilderness. These are just a couple of the early experiences that awakened these heroes' interest in the natural world.

They made important scientific discoveries.
In addition to being nature-lovers, these heroes were also dedicated scientists. From glaciers to trees, and from wolves to fruit flies, these men and women made valuable scientific discoveries. They combined their scientific understanding with their love of nature—head and heart working together—to protect wild places.

They shared their enthusiasm for nature with others.
These heroes didn't keep their love for Earth's wild places to themselves. They wrote and spoke about nature a lot. All together they wrote over 100 books! They've been called "speakers for the Earth" because they've given a voice to the natural world. Most were teachers and inspired thousands of students.

They helped shape the environmental movement.
The environmental movement consists of many different groups of people who want to preserve and protect the environment. Some believe the movement started in 1845, when Henry David Thoreau moved to Walden Pond. It continues to be led by people like David Suzuki and Wangari Maathai.

The ideas and actions of these Earth Heroes have made wild places available for all of us. Enjoy their exciting stories!

Earth Heroes: Champions of the Wilderness

Henry David Thoreau

1817-1862

Sage of Walden

"In wildness is the preservation of the world."

Henry stepped outside of his cabin door and gave a low whistle. A woodchuck immediately came out from its hiding place and approached. Then Henry gave another, different whistle, and a pair of gray squirrels scampered down the tree branches to his side. With yet another whistle, Henry called in several birds. A crow alighted on his shoulder. He fed each member of his "family" from the bits of food he kept in his pocket. Then, after gently petting them, he signaled each of them to leave with three unique, low, short whistles. Like students responding to the school bell, they left as quickly as they had come.

The wild birds and animals living on the edge of Walden Pond had come to know and trust Henry. For many days he patiently observed them, and they had lost their fear of him.

He was named David Henry when he was born on July 12, 1817; but he reversed the names, and the world knows him as Henry David Thoreau. Henry's mother nurtured a love of nature in him as she did all of her children. She would take them on long walks in the woods and meadows around their home in Concord, Massachusetts. As they walked, she taught them to identify bird songs and find the best places to pick huckleberries. Walden Pond and its surrounding woods, less than two miles from Henry's house, became one of the family's favorite places to visit. They would walk through the pine and maple trees and have picnics on the sandy shore of the pond. Of course, as a little boy of four, Henry had no idea that Walden Pond would play an important role in his adult life.

Henry was a nonconformist from the time he was a young boy. Preferring to stand on the sidelines, he didn't join in the games the other children were playing at school. When he was invited to the home of one of the most prominent families in Concord, other people considered it quite an honor. Not Henry. He refused to go. He didn't care about prestige or popularity. Although he had a good sense of humor, he was so quiet and solemn his classmates called him the "Judge." Even as a college student at Harvard, other students thought he was odd. He didn't participate in after-class sports activities or join in pranks and mischief. Henry's idea of fun was reading or being outside in nature.

Fortunately, Henry's family accepted him just as he was. His mother and aunts showered him with affection, sweetly calling him "our Henry." His older brother, John, was Henry's best friend. When they were young, the two boys loved to explore the Concord River. They imagined themselves building a boat and sailing off on exciting adventures—something they actually did when they were older. Another favorite place they investigated was Walden Woods. They would spend hours running barefoot, climbing trees, and tracking and hunting animals. Henry was alert and bold as he roamed through the trees, always ready for new experiences. Recalling his boyhood, Henry wrote that it was a "joyous time of discovery in nature."

As he grew older, he stopped hunting animals—he observed them instead. He believed that although a child's first introduction to the forest may be through hunting and fishing, there comes a time to leave the gun and fishing pole behind.

Henry's family wasn't wealthy. His mother turned their home into a boarding house to bring in additional money so that she could give her children the best education. Henry had dance and music lessons, attended private school, and eventually went to college. Their home was a bustling place filled with lots of noise and activity as boarders and relatives would come and go. Mrs. Thoreau had a zest for life and loved to talk. Their dinnertime conversations bubbled over with gossip and storytelling.

Henry's boyhood home was a lively place, busy with boarders and relatives.

In contrast to his mother, Henry's father was soft-spoken and quiet. After several business failures, he started a pencil-making factory where Henry worked from time to time as an adult. Henry used his creativity to make improvements in the production process. He devised a way to mix the graphite with a special clay to make a dark, high-quality lead. Thoreau pencils became highly valued for their superiority. Later, Henry converted the pencil factory to an ink factory, using graphite to make the ink. Some say that Henry could have become the "King of Graphite" in New England, but business didn't appeal to him. He thought that people should only work one day a week and spend six days as they pleased. For Henry, that meant reading, writing, and observing nature.

Throughout his life Henry yearned for freedom from work obligations. However, he was practical enough to realize that he had to earn a living to support himself. At the time, it was thought that college-educated men like Henry had only four career options: teacher, minister, lawyer, or doctor. Henry chose to become a teacher.

His first teaching job only lasted two weeks because of a disagreement with the school board. The board told Henry to use corporal punishment when students misbehaved; whipping was the standard disciplinary procedure in the 1830s. Henry preferred talking to his students rather than hitting them, so he left.

When he couldn't find another job, Henry opened his own private school with his brother, John, in 1838. They taught traditional subjects, but applied innovative teaching strategies. For example, Henry taught mathematics in a practical way, using surveying equipment. Both brothers took the class on field trips to local businesses and out into nature. The children were amazed at Henry's knowledge of the woods and rivers. He would often pull his magnifying glass from his pocket to give the children a closer look at a plant or flower. He had a knack for finding arrowheads and enthralled the class with stories about the Indians who used to live around Concord.

During their walks through the woods, Henry would also share his philosophy of life. True to his independent spirit, he cautioned the students to keep their minds open. He urged them to think out problems for themselves rather than relying on other people's solutions. He said, "What everybody echoes as true today may turn out to be falsehood tomorrow."

In 1839, when the school was closed for summer vacation, Henry and John took the river trip they had dreamed of as boys. Traveling in a 15-foot rowboat that they built themselves, they took "nature's nearest pathway" from Concord to New Hampshire and back. It was a happy time of adventure for both of them. They rushed over rapids and slept out under the stars. Henry kept a journal of the trip, and he used these notes to write his first book, *A Week on the Concord and Merrimack Rivers*. The book became a special tribute to John, who died in 1842.

Henry and John's school was a big success. Before the end of the first year they had a waiting list of students who wanted to attend. However, by 1841 John became too sick to teach. Henry decided that he didn't want to run the school on his own. When interviewed as adults, the students fondly remembered their teachers and said that Henry had opened their eyes to the beauty and wonder of nature.[1]

While Henry was teaching, he was also developing a deep friendship with Ralph Waldo Emerson, a well-respected philosopher, writer, and orator who had moved to Concord. In college Henry had read Emerson's book *Nature*. He was impressed by Emerson, especially his thoughts about man's relationship to God and nature. Emerson also admired Henry's independent spirit and willingness to live by his convictions. Not long after their first meeting in 1838 Emerson wrote in his journal, "I delight much in my young friend, who seems to have as free and erect a mind as any I have ever seen."[2]

Henry became a regular visitor to Emerson's home where he participated in intellectual discussions with Emerson's friends who called themselves "Transcendentalists." The Transcendentalists included authors, poets, and philosophers such as Amos Bronson Alcott, Nathanial Hawthorne, and Margaret Fuller. They believed in independence and self-reliance as they looked for deeper meanings of life. They thought that each person had a true "inner voice" that quietly reflected the soul. And they believed that being in nature was a way to more clearly hear that voice.

Henry and his brother, John, built a rowboat and rowed to New Hampshire and back. The trip was the subject of Henry's first book.

When Henry needed a job, Emerson hired him as a handyman and invited him to live with his family for a while. When there, Henry tutored Emerson's children, who grew to love him. A few years later, when Emerson went away on a long European lecture tour, Henry once again stayed at Emerson's home. One of his favorite pastimes was exploring Emerson's large library. He discovered new and interesting books, such as the *Bhagavad Gita*, a spiritual book from India. It inspired him and reinforced many of his beliefs.

Emerson recognized Henry's potential as a writer and encouraged him, saying, "Look in your heart and write."[3] Emerson edited a Transcendentalist magazine called *The Dial*, and he published some of Henry's essays. He also introduced Henry to literary critics and publishers in New York. When Henry wanted to go off by himself to think, write, and observe nature, Emerson generously offered him the use his property on Walden Pond. The spot was perfect for Henry. With the help of his friends, he built a tiny, one-room cabin under the pines on the shore of the pond, and moved in on Independence Day, July 4, 1845.

Today, Henry is famously remembered for the book he wrote while he lived at the pond—*Walden, or A Life in the Woods*. The book began as a lecture he planned to give so that he could explain to his neighbors why he moved there. Henry wrote:

> I went to the woods because I wished to live life deliberately, to confront only the essential facts of life, and see if I could not learn what it had to teach, and not, when I came to die, discover that I had not lived . . . . I wanted to live deep and suck out all the marrow of life . . . .

Walden is filled with Henry's enthusiasm for nature. "Our village life would stagnate if it were not for the unexplored forests and meadows which surround it. We need the tonic of wildness. . . . We can never have enough of nature." But *Walden* is more than just a nature book. It contains mythology, history, and poetry. In it Henry shared his knowledge of plants, wildlife, carpentry, and especially his philosophy about how to live freely, creatively, and in spiritual peace.

Henry built a one-room cabin at Walden Pond. He lived there alone for over two years.

Henry's cabin had three chairs: "one for solitude, two for friendship, three for society."

Henry thought most people cluttered their lives with too many things. Living by his principle of simplicity, Henry furnished his cabin with only a bed, a table, a desk, a few utensils, a tiny mirror, and three chairs—"one for solitude, two for friendship, three for society." Henry took his baths by swimming in Walden Pond and often cooked his meals over a fire outside. To earn a little money Henry did odd jobs and sold some of the beans from the field he planted close to the cabin.

In the mornings Henry focused on his writing, and in the afternoons he walked. And he walked and walked. Emerson also said, "It was a pleasure and a privilege to walk with him. He knew the country like a fox or a bird, and passed through it as freely by paths of his own."[4]

Henry loved the solitude he had at Walden. He wrote, "I find it wholesome to be alone the greater part of the time . . . I love to be alone." But Henry wasn't a hermit. He also enjoyed seeing his friends and family. Every few days he would make the short walk into Concord to have dinner or tea with his family, the Emersons, or his dear friends the Alcotts. Visitors also came regularly to his cabin. His sisters would bring him pies baked by his mother. Bronson Alcott came every week, often bringing his children, including Louisa May who would later become famous for writing her own book, *Little Women*.

Henry left Walden Pond in the autumn of 1847 after living there for two years, two months, and two days. He said, "I left the woods for as good a reason as I went in. Perhaps it seemed to me that I had several more lives to live, and could not spare any more time for that one." Returning to Concord, Henry worked on his writing, gave lectures at the Concord Lyceum, took several short trips to Cape Cod and Maine, and helped support his family.

Henry became known as an excellent land surveyor and could have made it a full-time profession. But Henry continued to do what he loved most—observe and write about nature. Whenever he went out on a walk he took an old music book with him that he used to press plants. In his pockets he had his journal, a pencil, a small spyglass for birds, a microscope, a jackknife, and some twine.

During the 1850s Henry focused more and more on his writing. He edited and polished his journal entries, which became the basis for several lectures and essays. Henry also increased the intensity of his nature study and research. He studied ferns, moss, and trees. He filled his notebooks with the dates when the birds arrived and the flowers bloomed. In 1860, he made a major contribution to the field of science with his lecture "The Succession of Trees." Like many of his lectures, he expanded it into a longer essay. This one was titled "The Dispersion of

Seeds", and it disproved the widely accepted theory of the time that some plants would spring spontaneously to life without beginning from a seed, root, or cutting.

Looking at the world with a questioning mind, Henry discovered things that others took for granted. When he saw the shadows of clouds in a valley, he calculated their height. When he observed a pattern made by fungi, he figured out why it formed the way it did. When he noticed that turtles buried their eggs three inches deep in the ground, Henry used thermometers to determine that both the day and night temperatures were greatest at that depth. Ellery Channing, one of Henry's closest friends, described him as being "alive from top to toe with curiosity."[5]

Always the nonconformist, Henry did things his own way. He walked at night when everyone else was sleeping. He took off his clothes and walked upstream through the river for the pure enjoyment of it. One morning, a local farmer saw him standing motionless on the edge of a little pond. At noon, Henry was still standing in the same spot. After dinner, Henry was still there. When the farmer asked what he was doing, Henry replied that he was studying bullfrogs. The farmer was flabbergasted that someone would spend an entire day just looking at frogs in a muddy pond! It was events like this one that led many of his neighbors and townspeople to call him a "loafer." They wondered: Why wasn't he working? But Henry ignored them. He thought that observing and recording natural events was serious work.

Often Henry would choose a destination and then, using only a compass, he would take off in a perfectly straight line—a beeline—for the spot. He would go over hills and mountains, through forests and meadows, across rivers and streams, not letting any obstacle stand in his way. Once when he was on a mountaintop in Maine, the fog became so thick he couldn't see his hand in front of him. That wasn't a problem for Henry. Earlier he had taken a reading with his compass, and he was able to lead his companions safely down the mountainside. Legend has it that during one of Henry's beeline hikes, a farmhouse stood in his way. Fortunately, both the front and back doors were open, so Henry stayed on his direct course and walked straight through the house.[6]

Even though the people of Concord didn't always understand Henry's eccentric ways, they came to realize how much he knew about the natural history of the area. Children as well as adults would bring him birds, bugs, nests, and eggs and Henry would identify them. Occasionally he would keep an unusual find and add it to the growing collection of natural treasures he had on display in his bedroom. He was especially good at answering children's questions, patiently explaining such mysteries as how a snake swallowed its prey or why rocks formed piles on the bottom of the river.

One of the young boys who visited Henry became so interested in natural history that he later became an official observer for the Smithsonian Institution. Another child said, "He first opened to our unconscious eyes a thousand beauties of the earth and air, and taught us to admire and appreciate all that was impressive and beautiful in the natural world around us."[7]

In December of 1860, Henry was researching trees. He lay on the cold, damp ground in Walden Woods so that he could count the tree rings of an old stump and caught a severe cold. His health declined until finally he realized he was dying from tuberculosis, a disease he had struggled with his entire adult life. Henry's friends came to his bedside to see him. When one person tried to console him, Henry replied, "When I was a boy I learned that I must die, so I'm not disappointed now . . . ."[8] Wanting to get several of his essays ready for publication, he worked on his writing whenever he had enough strength. He died on May 6, 1862, at the age of forty-four. Emerson's words at Henry's funeral were certainly true at the time, "The country knows not yet, or in the least part, how great a son it has lost."

Appreciation for Henry's work grew after his death, and several of his essays and journal excerpts were published posthumously. His words

Henry David Thoreau

17

and the example of his life have had a profound impact on history. Today Henry is considered one of the greatest American authors.

His writings formed the foundation for the environmental movement. He influenced early naturalists such as John Muir and John Burroughs, who in turn inspired many others to love and appreciate nature through their own writings. Henry watched civilization expanding into the countryside and warned that each town should have a primitive forest of 500 to 1000 acres where no trees were ever cut down. Such a forest would be used only for instruction and recreation.

Henry's influence also extended into the world of social justice. In his essay *Civil Disobedience*, Henry said that a man should follow his own conscience rather than unjust laws. Henry spoke out against slavery and even went to jail for refusing to pay a tax because he didn't support the U.S. government's involvement in the Mexican War. Mahatma Gandhi applied Henry's principles when he created a civil disobedience movement that brought about India's independence from British rule. Martin Luther King, Jr. used these same ideas in the U.S. during the civil rights movement of the 1960s.

Henry David Thoreau didn't seek fame. Yet every year visitors from around the world travel to Concord and Walden Pond to see where he lived and walked. His words are quoted by presidents and nature lovers. They appear in textbooks and on t-shirts. Many of them are as meaningful today as when Henry wrote them. They include:

An early-morning walk is a blessing for the whole day.

Do not worry if you have built your castles in the air. They are where they should be. Now put the foundations under them.

If a man does not keep pace with his companions, perhaps it is because he hears a different drummer. Let him step to the music which he hears, however measured or far away.

Success usually comes to those who are too busy to be looking for it.

Friends…cherish one another's hopes. They are kind to one another's dreams.

Go confidently in the direction of your dreams. Live the life you have imagined.

Heaven is under our feet as well as over our heads.

I would rather sit on a pumpkin and have it all to myself, than be crowded on a velvet cushion.

It is not enough to be busy. So are the ants. The question is: What are we busy about?

Simplicity, simplicity, simplicity!

What is the use of a house if you haven't got a tolerable planet to put it on?

It's not what you look at that matters, it's what you see.

This world is but a canvas to our imagination.

The bluebird carries the sky on his back.

FAST FACTS

Born: July 12, 1817, Concord, Massachusetts
Died: May 6, 1862, Concord, Massachusetts
Family: Mother, father, brother, two sisters

ACCOMPLISHMENTS:
- One of the greatest American authors
- Formed the basis for the environmental movement with his writings
- Defender of social justice
- His observations are currently being used in the study of climate change.

RIPPLES OF INFLUENCE:

Famous People who Influenced Henry David Thoreau
Ralph Waldo Emerson, Amos Bronson Alcott, Nathaniel Hawthorne, Ellery Channing, Charles Darwin, John Brown.
He was also influenced by his mother, who introduced him to the natural world when very young.

Famous People who Henry David Thoreau Influenced
John Muir, John Burroughs, Mahatma Gandhi, Martin Luther King, Jr., Frank Lloyd Wright, Sinclair Lewis, John F. Kennedy

TIMELINE OF IMPORTANT EVENTS

Henry David Thoreau's Life		Historical Context
Born July 12	1817	
	1820	The Missouri Compromise
	1833	The word "scientist" is coined
Graduates from Harvard; meets Emerson	1837	Queen Victoria begins her reign
Opens a private school with his brother	1838	John Muir is born
Takes a boat trip with his brother	1839	Daguerre invents first form of photography
Publishes poems and essays in *The Dial*	1840	
	1840-1860	Pioneers travel the Oregon Trail
Moves into Emerson's home	1841	
Tutors children in New York	1843	
Improves the process for making pencils	1844	Dumas writes *The Three Musketeers*
Moves to Walden Pond	1845	
Spends night in jail for not paying taxes	1846	
Leaves Walden Pond	1847	
	1848	Gold is discovered in California
Works as surveyor; writes in journal	1850	Hawthorne writes *The Scarlet Letter*
Spends a "year of observation" in nature	1853	
Publishes *Walden, or, Life in the Woods*	1854	
	1855	Whitman writes *Leaves of Grass*
	1858	Theodore Roosevelt is born
Manages the pencil factory; lectures	1859	Darwin publishes *The Origin of Species*
Catches a bad cold while studying trees	1860	
	1861-1864	U.S. Civil War
Dies May 6	1862	

John Muir
1838–1914

Speaker for the Wilderness

"Climb the mountains and get their good tidings. Nature's peace will flow into you as sunshine flows into trees. The winds will blow their own freshness into you, and the storms their energy, while cares will drop off like autumn leaves."

Every few minutes another huge tree crashed to the ground. Leaves and branches flew through the air as a storm raged through the mountains of California. Some trees were completely uprooted. Others broke straight across. The tops of flexible, young sugar pines bent completely to the ground from the force of the gale. Most people hovered near their fireplaces on that December morning in 1874, but not John Muir.

John was energized by it. He set off into it, delighted by the "music" the trees made as they wildly arced across the sky. Listening intently, John could distinguish the sounds of the pines from those of the spruce, the fir, and the oaks. Exhilarated, John climbed to the top of a 100-foot tall Douglas fir. Later he wrote, "Never before did I enjoy so noble an exhilaration of motion. The slender top fairly flapped and swished in the passionate torrent, bending and swirling backward and forward, round and round . . . while I clung with muscles firm braced, like a bobolink on a reed."[1]

John Muir thrived on wilderness adventures, and he was passionate about protecting the wilderness. Although he may be most famous as a great environmentalist and founder of the Sierra Club, he described himself as "a tramp." He was also an inventor, writer, friend to presidents and philosophers, farmer, geologist, glaciologist and lecturer, as well as a husband and a father.

John Muir's love of nature was nurtured by his grandfather, who took him for short walks around the countryside near his home in Dunbar, Scotland. Even at the age of three, John's senses were keen. On one excursion he heard tiny cries coming from a mound of hay in the field. John dug through the hay to reveal a mother mouse nursing her babies. John loved to taste fresh figs in summer and study the lilies in his aunt's garden. These early tendencies were echoed in his later life when he described in exquisite detail the animals he observed in the wilderness and when he managed a large orchard business.

John later wrote in his autobiography that he and his friends

> . . . loved to wander in the fields to hear the birds sing, and along the seashore to gaze and wonder at the shells and seaweeds, eels and crabs in the pools among the rocks when the tide was low; and best of all to watch the waves in awful storms thundering on the black headlands and craggy ruins of old Dunbar Castle . . . .[2]

The castle was one of John's favorite destinations. He developed his mountaineering skills on it as he ran, jumped, and climbed on its crags and walls, pretending to be a heroic Scottish warrior of old.

John and his friends competed to see who could find the most birds' nests. It wasn't unusual for someone to find over twenty nests. Their most treasured bird was the skylark. John declared, "No Scotch boy that I know of ever failed to listen with enthusiasm to the songs of the skylarks. Oftentimes on a broad meadow near Dunbar we stood for hours enjoying their marvelous singing and soaring."[3] The boys would test their eyesight by watching skylarks fly high into the sky until the birds disappeared beyond their vision.

John loved challenges and would play games of daring, which he and his friends called "scootchers." One summer night, in search of a good scootcher, John climbed out of the dormer window in his bedroom. He held onto the windowsill as he hung his body over the roof slates. He dared his brother, David, to do the same. David did it successfully. Then John hung by just one hand—and David did the same. Then John hung by one finger, and again David did it too.

To make the next challenge more difficult, John climbed up the steep roof, using the tiny spaces between the slates as fingerholds. Sitting astride the rooftop, he looked at the scenery below as the wind howled, threatening to blow him off. He then slid down the slippery slates, caught hold of the windowsill, and pulled himself back into the bedroom. Not to be outdone, David attempted the same feat. But he lost his courage once he got to the top of the roof. John rescued him by crawling out onto the roof, catching hold of David's feet, and miraculously pulling him inside.

Upon visiting his Dunbar home fifty years later, John commented on this scootcher:

> I obtained permission to go upstairs to visit our bedroom window and judge what sort of adventure getting on its roof must have been, and with all my after experience in mountaineering I found that what I had done in daring boyhood was now beyond my skill.[4]

In the wintertime, John and David would amuse themselves by playing a fantasy game they called "voyages around the world" under the bedcovers. They imagined themselves visiting faraway India, Australia, New Zealand, and America. Little did John know that he would actually visit these and many other countries during his long life.

John's father, however, had different ideas. He wanted him to remain close to home. He sternly demanded that John stay in the back yard or garden. But despite the severe punishment that he was sure to get, John repeatedly ignored his father's strict orders and scrambled over the garden wall to join his friends on wild escapades. He was thrilled by the "fullness of Nature's glad wildness" and referred to his boyhood excursions as the beginnings of his lifelong wanderings.

When John was eleven years old his family moved to the New World. John loved the rushing wind and turbulent waves of the ocean voyage, even though most of the passengers suffered from seasickness. While aboard ship, John's father had heard that Wisconsin was good for farming, so he bought land near the town of Portage.

For the next eleven years, John's life was filled with strenuous labor. During the summer he worked from four in the morning until nine at night clearing land, plowing fields, digging wells, and harvesting crops. Even when he was sick with the mumps, his father expected him to put in a full day's work. All of the Muir children suffered under their father's harsh discipline, but as the oldest boy, the heaviest burdens fell on John.

In spite of all the work, John loved the Wisconsin wilderness and delighted in discovering the plants and animals in the woods, meadows, marshes, and lakes that surrounded his new home. He called the openings in the oak forest a "paradise for birds" and felt a deep appreciation for robins, jays, nuthatches, thrushes, geese, cranes, bluebirds, blackbirds, and all of the many other birds he came to know and love.

When he was about fifteen years old, he discovered another love—a love for learning. He easily mastered algebra and advanced mathematics and along the way developed an interest in literature and poetry. Because his father demanded that he go to bed immediately after evening prayers with the rest of family, which in winter was at eight o'clock, John only had time to snatch a few minutes for reading. It was never enough.

John repeatedly asked to stay up later, but he was always told "No." Finally his father gave him permission to get up as early in the morning as he liked. When John woke up the next morning he didn't know how early it was until he held his candle to the clock. To his surprise, it was only one o'clock in the morning. He had five whole hours before he had to go to work in the snowy woods. Recalling that morning he later wrote, "I can hardly think of any other event in my life, any discovery I ever made that gave birth to joy so transportingly glorious as the possession of these five frosty hours."[5]

And "frosty" they were! John's father barely kept the house heated during the day and not at all at night. It was freezing inside—too cold for reading. So John went to the slightly warmer cellar below the house and began tinkering. He had thought of an invention, a self-set sawmill, and wanted to build it. When he realized that he didn't have the tools he needed, he made them from materials he could find. After finishing the sawmill, creative ideas kept coming to him. He invented many unique gadgets and machines including waterwheels, complicated door locks and latches, thermometers, hygrometers, and pyrometers. One of the most unusual inventions was an alarm clock that operated a bed. At a given hour, the clock would strike and the bed would be raised so the person sleeping in it would be dumped out onto the floor! John called it an early-rising machine.

Although John didn't get any support from his father, a kind neighbor recognized John's talent and encouraged him to take his inventions to the

State Agricultural Fair in Madison. John had been agonizing over what he should do with his life, so he followed his neighbor's advice. At the fair, people marveled at his inventions, and John won a prize of $15.

Always wanting to learn more, John became a student at the University of Wisconsin. His life in Madison was rich in new experiences, influences, and friendships. He learned about some of the great thinkers of that time including the scientist Louis Agassiz, the philosopher Ralph Waldo Emerson, and the author/naturalist Henry David Thoreau.

Jeanne Carr, the wife of one of John's favorite professors, had been one of the judges at the fair. She saw something special in John and took an interest in him. The Carr home was a haven for John, "filled with books, peace, kindliness, and patience," and Jeanne became a lifelong friend and mentor.

The mechanical desk John invented.

One of John's most significant botany lessons came outside of class from a fellow student named Milton Griswold. By comparing a locust tree to a pea vine, Griswold introduced John to the world of botanical classification. John was amazed at the similarities between two such different plants. For the first time his eyes were opened to seeing the universal patterns of nature. The two friends spent many hours sorting and classifying the plants they found.

While at the university, John continued inventing things. For example, he was always looking for ways to be more efficient, so he created a desk to help him study. The desk would pull out a book, lay it open for reading for a specified amount of time, then pick it up and replace it with the next book to be read. His room became a magnet that drew people to see his wonderful devices. Years later, stories about John's inventions were still being talked about around the campus.

Although he enjoyed his classes, John's other love—the wilderness— kept calling him. And when the first flowers bloomed in the spring of 1864, he took off, wandering throughout northeast Canada, studying plants and adding new flowers and ferns to his growing collection. Later in life he said that he had left Wisconsin University for the "University of the Wilderness."

John didn't know what he should do with his life. For a time he worked in a rake and broom factory where he invented machines to increase production. When the factory burned down, John moved to Indianapolis, Indiana. He took another factory job there, planning to stay only long enough to earn enough money to continue his wanderings. But the factory boss recognized his skill for inventing, and John's position in the company rose along with his salary. He made good friends in Indianapolis, as he did wherever he went, but he felt an inner conflict. He loved inventing and enjoyed the happy times with friends, but he also loved roaming solitary and free in the wilderness.

Then a serious accident shaped his life's direction forever. One night he was working late at the factory when a file slipped from his fingers and hit him in the right eye. As the fluid drained from his eye, he exclaimed, "My right eye gone! Closed forever on all God's beauty!" John also lost sight in his left eye as well for a while, due to nerve damage and in sympathy with his right eye. Blind! He was disconsolate. He spent a month in a dark room, dreaming day and night of the wilderness.

Finally, one month after the accident, his eyes healed—he could see again! Within hours of his first walk outside, he made an important decision. He would follow the persistent longing in his heart for the wilderness. He felt good about this decision because he knew he was being true to himself. He could never be truly happy if he was separated from wild nature.

On September 1, 1867, at the age of twenty-nine, John set off on a long walk, not knowing where he would eventually end up. His address? As he wrote in his journal: John Muir, Earth-Planet, Universe.

And John walked. He walked a thousand miles to the Gulf of Mexico. He walked through the desolation in the South left by the Civil War. He walked among the alligators in the Florida swamps. He walked and walked. After surviving malaria, John took a ship to California. When he arrived in the city of San Francisco, he asked a man the nearest way out of town. "But where do you want to go?" the man asked. John replied, "To any place that is wild."

John continued his walking across California's great central valley to the Sierra Nevada Mountains—a place he would call the Range of Light. He was awed by the beauty of the mountains and stayed in Yosemite for six years. John worked at various jobs—sawyer, sheepherder, ranch hand, and guide. These kinds of jobs suited him because they gave him lots of time to wander in the wilderness and contemplate nature. He filled his journals with detailed descriptions and sketches of everything he was seeing and feeling. One journal passage reads, "Exhilarated with the mountain air, I feel like shouting this morning with excess of wild animal joy."

The plants, animals, rock, trees, and rivers became his teachers, and his wilderness philosophy began to emerge as he felt an underlying unity and harmony in all of nature. He wrote, "When we try to pick out anything by itself, we find it hitched to everything else in the Universe."[6] And:

> Wonderful how completely everything in wild nature fits into us, as if truly part and parent of us. The sun shines not on us but in us. The rivers flow not past, but through us, thrilling, tingling, vibrating every fiber and cell of the substance of our bodies, making them glide and sing. The trees wave and the flowers bloom in our bodies as well as our souls, and every bird song, wind song, and tremendous storm song of

John walked a thousand miles from Indiana to Florida, where he took a ship to San Francisco. From there he walked to the Sierra Nevada Mountains.

John Muir

the rocks in the heart of the mountains is our song, our very own, and sings our love.

John delighted in introducing like-minded friends to his favorite places. He took artist William Keith and two companions on a trip to the middle of the Sierras, and while they sketched a panoramic scene, John set out by himself to climb Mt. Ritter. No one had been able to climb to the summit, and John wanted to give it a try. John carefully zigzagged up the sheer face of the mountain. But when he was only about halfway to the top he realized that he couldn't find any more cracks or fissures in the granite to use as handholds. With his arms completely outstretched, he clung to the sheer face of the rock unable to move in any direction. He was overcome by the danger of his situation. Suddenly, what he called his "other self" took over.[7] He had a strange surge of strength and his sight was magnified as if he were looking through a microscope. He was able to see places in the rock for him to put his hands and feet, and miraculously began climbing again. When John reached the top of the mountain he leapt for joy!

Based on his personal observations, John developed an explanation about how the Yosemite Valley was carved out by glaciers. Although his ideas are now accepted as fact, in 1871 they were quite controversial. Glaciers fascinated John, and he took several trips to Alaska to study them. A magnificent glacier he discovered in Glacier Bay carries his name—the Muir Glacier.

The topic of John's first public lecture was glaciers. Feeling shy and uncomfortable speaking to a large group of people, John's talk began terribly. Fortunately, his artist friend William Keith had given him good advice along with a painting of a majestic mountain scene. Keith told John that he should look at the painting during his talk if he was nervous. The strategy worked! As soon as John looked at the painting, all his fears vanished and his words flowed easily. His lecture was a huge hit. Even though he became a popular and inspiring speaker, one of his friends said that John always preferred "wild beasts to a formal audience."[8]

When Ralph Waldo Emerson arrived in Yosemite in 1871, John was beside himself with excitement. However, he was reluctant to actually meet someone he admired so much. Later John would say, "So great was my awe and reverence, I did not dare to go to him or speak to him." Finally, John got up his nerve, and he and Emerson spent several happy days together. This first meeting was the beginning of many years of correspondence and a deep friendship. They shared a mutual admiration for each other, and Emerson added John Muir's name to the list of the greatest men he had ever met.

While John was in Yosemite, his dear friends Jeanne Carr and her husband moved from Madison, Wisconsin, to nearby Oakland. Jeanne continued to guide John as she had done when he was a student. She influenced two key events in John's life: she introduced him to Louisa Strentzel, who became his wife, and she advised him to become an author so that he could share his love of nature with others.

Water Ouzel

Although John was a reluctant author, he became the voice for the wilderness through his writings. Readers were enchanted by his stories of wild adventures, and fell in love with the cheerful water ouzel and the giant sequoias he wrote about so enthusiastically.

He wrote, "Everybody needs beauty as well as bread, places to play in and pray in, where Nature may heal and cheer and give strength to body and soul." His books and magazine articles not only enticed people to see nature's loveliness, but also persuaded them to preserve wild places. Magazine editor Robert Underwood Johnson asserted that "Muir's writings and enthusiasm were the chief forces that inspired the conservation movement. All other torches were lighted from

John and President Theodore Roosevelt on a four-day camping trip in Yosemite.

his."[9] He's been called "The Father of our National Parks," "Wilderness Prophet," and "Citizen of the Universe."

John constantly wrote letters to politicians and policy makers, extolling the importance of preserving the wilderness. He became the first president of the Sierra Club, a watchdog organization dedicated to protecting wilderness lands. In 1903 he took President Theodore Roosevelt on a four-day camping trip in Yosemite. Roosevelt said,

> Lying out at night under those giant sequoias was lying in a temple built by no hand of man, a temple grander than any human architect

could by any possibility build, and I hope for the preservation of the groves of giant trees simply because it would be a shame to our civilization to let them disappear. They are monuments in themselves.[10]

By the end of his presidency Roosevelt had added land to Yosemite National Park and created five new national parks, 55 wildlife preserves, and 150 national forests.

John became worn down in body and spirit with the constant writing and lecturing. When exhausted, he would retreat for a little while to the wilderness; it gave him physical strength and peace of mind. His wife and two daughters supported John in taking this time to himself. And his childhood wishes came true as he traveled the world, thrilling to the sights of the baobab trees in Africa, the flowers of New Zealand, and the Himalayan Mountains in India.

Although John's writings had enormous influence, not all of his environmental campaigns were successful. He disagreed with Gifford Pinchot, the first chief of the Forest Service, who favored using the wilderness resources for people and for profit. One of John's fiercest battles was trying to preserve the Hetch Hetchy Valley, a place he compared in beauty to Yosemite Valley. Despite John's valiant efforts, the Tuolumne River was dammed, flooding the Hetch Hetchy Valley so it could be used as a water reservoir for San Francisco residents. Although it was a heartbreaking defeat, his close friend Mrs. Parsons wrote, "No trace of pessimism or despondency, even in the defeat of his most deeply cherished hopes, ever darkened his beautiful philosophy . . . ."[11]

To the end of his life John continued to write. He died on Christmas Eve 1914, spending his last days with his daughters. Many of his books and articles were published after his death, and John's influence on the environmental movement is still much alive. John's birthday, April 21st, has been proclaimed in California as John Muir Day—a day set aside to honor the man who helped others to see the significance and beauty of the wilderness and to realize that it should be protected for future generations.

FAST FACTS

Born: April 21, 1838 in Dunbar, Scotland

Died: December 24, 1914 in Los Angeles, California

Wife: Louisa Strentzel

Daughters: Wanda and Helen

ACCOMPLISHMENTS:
- Created many unique inventions
- Explored Yosemite and the Sierras
- Influenced the creation of the National Park System
- One of the founders of the Sierra Club
- Influential writer on conservation and preservation

RIPPLES OF INFLUENCE:

Famous People who Influenced John Muir
Robert Burns, Jeanne Carr, Ralph Waldo Emerson, Henry David Thoreau, Louis Agassiz, Asa Gray, Joseph LeConte, William Keith, John Swett, John Burroughs. He was also influenced by his grandfather.

Famous People who John Muir Influenced
President Theodore Roosevelt, Aldo Leopold, Ansel Adams, Ryozo Asuma, David Brower, Enos Mills, Sigurd Olson

John drew his self-portrait and said, "Someone looking at me would see two eyes, like small open spots on a hillside."

Earth Heroes: Champions of the Wilderness

TIMELINE OF IMPORTANT EVENTS

John Muir's Life		Historical Context
Born April 21	1838	
	1848	Gold is discovered in California
Moves to Wisconsin	1849	
	1854	Thoreau writes *Walden*
	1858	Theodore Roosevelt is born
Goes to Wisconsin Fair	1860	
	1861-1864	U.S. Civil War
Travels in Canada	1864-1866	
Begins 1000-mile walk	1867	Alfred Nobel patents dynamite
Spends his first summer in the Sierra	1869	Suez Canal opens
Meets Ralph Waldo Emerson in Yosemite	1871	
Climbs Mt. Ritter	1872	Lewis Carroll writes *Through the Looking-Glass*
Climbs fir tree to experience winter storm	1874	
Gives first public lecture	1876	Alexander Graham Bell invents telephone
Takes first trip to Alaska	1879	Edison invents incandescent electric light
Helps establish Yosemite as a National Park	1880	
	1885	Louis Pasteur creates rabies vaccination
	1887	Aldo Leopold is born
Becomes president of the Sierra Club	1892	
	1902	Margaret "Mardy" Murie is born
Camps with Theodore Roosevelt in Yosemite	1903	Wright Brothers fly airplane
	1906	The Great San Francisco Earthquake
Begins fight to save Hetch Hetchy Valley	1907	
	1908	Muir Woods National Monument declared
Publishes *Stickeen*	1909	NAACP forms in New York City
	1910	British Empire covers 1/5 of world's land area
Travels around the world	1911-1912	
Loses the battle to save Hetch Hetchy Valley	1913	
Dies December 24	1914	World War I begins in Europe
	1916	National Park System is established

John Muir

37

Earth Heroes: Champions of the Wilderness

Theodore Roosevelt

1858-1919

The Conservation President

"There can be no greater issue than that of conservation in this country."

Seven-year-old Theodore Roosevelt pushed his way through the crowded market street in New York City. There on a wooden slab was a dead seal. Teddy had never seen such a creature before. It fascinated him. Day after day he went back to study it. He carefully measured it and made notes about his observations. Then one day the shopkeeper gave him the skull to take home. What a prize!

The seal skull became the first specimen in the "Roosevelt Natural History Museum," which Teddy established in his bedroom. Enthusiastically he added birds' nests, mice, insects, shells, turtles, and snakes to his collection. By the time he was eleven, his museum included over 250 specimens. Teddy continued to collect specimens his entire life. Some are still displayed in public museums.

As an adult, Teddy was an active outdoor adventurer, cowboy, soldier, and sportsman. But as a child he was "sickly and delicate."[1] He suffered from asthma, which made it difficult for him to breathe. He spent many nights propped up in a chair gasping for air. Today, doctors know how to treat and prevent asthma. But in the 1800s they didn't know what to do. Asthma was a life-threatening illness.

Teddy was an invalid for most of his early childhood. Then, when he was eleven, his father said, "You have the mind, but not the body, and without the help of the body, the mind cannot go as far as it should. You must *make* your body."[2]

Teddy greatly admired his father and would do anything to please him. From that moment on he spent long hours exercising. His father installed a gym in their house, and Teddy worked out every day. He lifted weights, swung on parallel bars, and did lots of sit-ups and chin-ups. After he was teased and bullied by a group of boys, he took boxing lessons so that he could defend himself in a fight. Although he was skinny and little, he had a lot of will power, discipline, and perseverance—qualities that he showed again and again throughout his life.

Teddy's father, nicknamed "Thee," influenced Teddy's life in another important way: he did a lot of public service. The Roosevelts were one of the wealthiest families in New York City, and Thee believed that he should use his money to do good works for others. He took personal responsibility for making the city a better place to live, spending most of his time working on civic and charity projects. He raised money to send orphans to farms in the Midwest and helped build the Young Men's Christian Association (YMCA). Thee also gave inspirational talks to the homeless boys at the local missions. He often took Teddy along with him on these visits.

In addition to helping the poor, Thee worked on cultural projects. He helped start the American Museum of Natural History and the Metropolitan Museum of Art, both of which are world-famous today. Throughout his life, Teddy followed in his father's footsteps by supporting projects that he believed were for the good of the American people.

In 1872, the Roosevelts took a trip to Europe and the Middle East. Teddy was fourteen. While cruising on the Nile River in Egypt, he saw many new and exotic birds. "Pages of his diary came alive with squawks and fluttering wings."[3]

A highlight of his trip was using his new gun. As the houseboat slowly made its way up the Nile, Teddy roamed along the shore and shot birds. He claimed that he shot 100 to 200.

Because he had studied taxidermy, he knew how to preserve them. His brother complained about smelly skins that filled their bedroom.

But Teddy collected wonderful specimens. Four of his Egyptian birds later appeared in the American Museum of Natural History. The Smithsonian Institution in Washington, D.C., accepted many of his other specimens.

Being a hunter might seem like a contradiction for a person like Teddy who loved birds and animals. However, during the 1800s and early 1900s, most naturalists were also hunters. They killed animals so they could carefully study them. Even the famous John James Audubon killed birds in order to accurately paint them for his book *Birds of North America*.

Teddy admires a macaw.

Teddy remained an enthusiastic hunter his entire life. One of his most famous hunting trips took place when he was President. He went to Mississippi to hunt bear. After three days of hunting he hadn't seen any, and the guides leading the trip didn't want the President to be disappointed. So they found an old bear and tied it to a tree. When they brought Teddy to the bear, he absolutely refused to shoot it. He told them he was a true sportsman. He would never shoot an animal that was tied to a tree!

A newspaper cartoonist drew a picture of the incident portraying the bear as a cute little cub. The adorable cartoon gave a shopkeeper an idea. He put two stuffed toy bears in his store window and called them "Teddy bears" in honor of the President. The name caught on! Teddy bears became a favorite toy of children everywhere.

Like many hunters, Teddy's experiences helped him appreciate nature. They also inspired him to protect it. In 1888, with several of his hunting friends, Teddy founded the Boone and Crockett Club. Club members wanted to preserve wild game. They knew they wouldn't be successful unless they also preserved the wilderness. The Boone and Crockett Club supported laws protecting the

lands and animals of Yellowstone National Park, saving the sequoia trees in California, and giving the President the power to create forest preserves.

As a teenager, Teddy was home-schooled by tutors. It gave him a lot of time to study animals in his own way. He continued his own style of learning when he went away to college at Harvard. He once again filled his room with specimens he collected near Boston.

During summer vacations, he explored the mountains of upstate New York. The science of bird identification interested him, and he gathered detailed data about each bird he collected. His notebooks were filled with Latin names followed by exact descriptions, sizes, weights, and wingspans. If he dissected a bird, he would write down the contents of its stomach. After several summers, he published a leaflet listing all the bird species he identified.

Teddy had a hard time deciding what to do after graduation. Although he wanted to become a naturalist, he finally chose to go to law school. Then he discovered his passion: politics. In 1881, he was elected to the New York State Assembly as a legislator from New York City. Teddy's lifelong political career was underway at the age of twenty-six.

He was enjoying his life as an assemblyman when tragedy struck. His wife, Alice, died just two days after giving birth to their first child. Sadly, Teddy's mother died of typhoid fever on the very same day. It was Valentine's Day, 1884.

Teddy was heartbroken. He didn't know how to cope with such a loss. Leaving his newborn daughter in the care of his older sister, he headed west to forget his sorrow. In a letter to his sister he said that he was going "far off from all mankind."[4]

He went to the Dakota Territory—an area called the "Badlands" which is now in the state of North Dakota. He bought land and cattle and enthusiastically immersed himself in ranch life. He rode horses, branded cattle, and camped out under the stars. In his autobiography Teddy wrote, "It was still the Wild West in those days. In that land we led a hardy life. Ours was the glory of work and the joy of living."[5] He hunted buffalo, elk, deer, grouse, ducks, and bighorn sheep. And wherever he went, he carefully observed the birds and animals.

Cowboy Teddy with his horse.

Theodore Roosevelt

The time he spent in the West had a huge impact on his life. He wrote about his experiences in three books that were filled with action, adventure, and glorious descriptions of plants and animals. For many years Teddy traveled back and forth between the East and the West. His appreciation for the West influenced many of his environmental policies when he later became President.

Although Teddy loved the land, he also loved politics. He quickly rose to higher and higher offices. He became New York City's Police Commissioner and then Assistant Secretary of the Navy. During the Spanish-American War, Teddy became a real war hero. He led a group of volunteers called the "Rough Riders" up San Juan Hill in Cuba. The newspapers loved writing about his brave actions, and he became extremely popular with the American people.

When he returned from the war, he was elected Governor of New York and then Vice President. When President McKinley was assassinated, Teddy, only forty-two years old, became the youngest President in the history of the United States. He served for the remaining three years of McKinley's term and was then elected President in his own right for four more years.

Always an adventurer, Teddy liked to be the first person to try something new. As President, his "firsts" included:

- flying in an airplane
- going underwater in a submarine
- owning a car
- having a telephone in his home
- traveling outside the borders of the US while still in office
  (He took the battleship USS Louisiana to Panama.)
- hosting an African-American in the White House
  (He invited Booker T. Washington to dinner.)
- winning a Nobel Prize

Teddy's "firsts" also included protecting nature. He created the first bird sanctuary, which began the Wildlife Refuge System. He also established the first 18 national monuments, including the Grand Canyon and Muir Woods. At his urging, Congress established the U.S. Forest Service as an agency for the care and management of forests and grasslands. By the end of his presidency, Teddy had protected millions of acres of land. He set aside more land in national parks and nature preserves than all of the previous presidents combined.

In his very first message to Congress he said, "The preservation of our forests is an imperative business necessity. We have come to see clearly that whatever destroys the forests, except to make way for agriculture, threatens our well-being."[6]

Even during his busy schedule he would make time for what he called "point to point" hikes in nearby Rock Creek Park. Ambassadors, congressmen, and other government officials tried to keep up with him

Teddy was an energetic statesman.

as he scrambled over, under, or through—but never around—boulders, tree trunks, bogs, and streams. Back at his desk in the White House, it wasn't unusual for him suddenly to stop in the middle of a conversation, run to the window, and scan the trees to see a songbird he heard singing.

Outside of Washington, Teddy had two favorite nature retreats: Sagamore Hill and Pine Knot. Sagamore Hill was the name of his home located on Oyster Bay, Long Island. When he was a child, Teddy spent many summers there. As an adult, it refreshed him to wander in the woods and see the birds and animals that he knew so well. Sagamore Hill was a spacious mansion that could accommodate his second wife, Edith, his six children, and many friends.

In contrast, Pine Knot was a small, rustic cabin—a secluded retreat in the Blue Ridge Mountains of Virginia. For Teddy it was the perfect place to get away from everything and everyone. Only his closest friends were allowed to visit.

One special visitor to Pine Knot was John Burroughs. He was a famous naturalist and writer. Like Teddy, he was an avid "birder." The two men were as excited as little boys as they took turns introducing each other to new species of birds.

In 1903, Burroughs joined Teddy on a trip to Yellowstone. They spent two wonderful weeks riding horseback and hiking. Teddy was delighted to see *all* of the wildlife, from a huge elk to a tiny field mouse. Burroughs later praised Teddy, saying, "The President is a born nature lover . . . and he has remarkable powers of observation."[7] He pointed out that although many people saw big things, Teddy keenly observed even little things.

After leaving Yellowstone, Teddy explored another beautiful national park, Yosemite, with another famous naturalist and writer, John Muir. The two men eagerly left the press behind and went camping for four days. They rode mules out into the woods, and Muir made a bed of ferns and branches so they could sleep outside under the giant sequoia trees. Teddy was delighted to wake up one morning with snow on his blanket!

Naturalist John Burroughs often visited Teddy at his Pine Knot retreat.

In many ways, John Muir and Teddy agreed about the importance of "wildness" in a person's life. "Mountains, trees, and glaciers were sacred temples to Muir, and Teddy sensed a deeper kinship with birds and animals than he did with many men." [8]

Both of Teddy's companions, Muir and Burroughs, were influential in getting Americans to take notice of the environment. They wrote about the wonders of nature and the danger of destroying natural resources. But many people continued to feel that the United States was so large that there would always be plenty of everything.

Teddy thought differently. He knew that many of the country's natural resources were being destroyed or wasted. With his own eyes he had seen vast forests disappear and rivers ruined by soil erosion. He saw buffalo shot for no reason and left for dead on the plains. So many were destroyed, they were in danger of becoming extinct. So were the white herons (egrets) that were being killed so their feathers could be used to decorate women's hats.

When Teddy returned to Washington after his trip to Yellowstone and Yosemite, he was even more passionate about saving the environment, game, and birds "for the people unborn." To voices like Muir and Burroughs he added his own. With the authority of the presidency he declared:

> Surely our people do not understand even yet the rich heritage that is theirs. There is nothing in the world more beautiful than the Yosemite, the groves of giant Sequoias and redwoods, the Canyon of the Colorado, the Canyon of the Yellowstone, the three Tetons; and the people should see to it that they are preserved for their children and their children's children forever, with their majestic beauty all unmarred.[9]

Teddy worked closely with Gifford Pinchot to establish environmental policies, and he made him the first head of the U.S. Forest Service. Pinchot believed that natural resources should be protected so that they would last a very long time. He thought the U.S. would continue to be a strong nation if its land and water were used wisely and effectively. He coined the term "conservation."

John Muir's ideas differed from Pinchot's. Muir didn't think nature's value was based on how resources could be used. He believed that people needed the wilderness as a place to go to renew their spirits. He believed in "preservation."

Although both men had the same goal of protecting the environment, they had different approaches for achieving that goal. When San Francisco proposed to dam the Tuolumne River at the Hetch Hetchy Valley, the whole country learned about the conflict between the "conservationists" and "preservationists."

Muir opposed building the dam. He called Hetch Hetchy "one of Nature's rarest and most precious mountain temples."[10] Because Hetch Hetchy was part of Yosemite National Park, it was protected by the government. It would take an act of Congress to allow the dam to be built.

Pinchot supported building the dam. A dam would allow water to be used by thousands of people in San Francisco. He said, "The benefits to be derived from use as a reservoir far outweigh the valley as a place of beauty."[11]

News of Hetch Hetchy filled the papers. For the first time many Americans began to think about what the environment meant to them. Did they agree with the conservationists or the preservationists? Teddy had to make a very difficult decision. He sided with Pinchot. Eventually, after many hearings and debates, the dam was built.

Teddy's term as president ended in 1909, but his enthusiasm for adventures in nature continued. The Smithsonian Institution sponsored him on a hunting trip to Africa to enlarge its natural history exhibits. Teddy brought back the largest collection of items from a single expedition. It included 5,013 mammals, 4,453 birds, 2,322 reptiles and amphibians, and thousands of fish, insects, shells, and plants.

In December of 1913, Teddy departed on his last major adventure: a trip into the unexplored jungles of Brazil to search for the source of a mystery river called the River of Doubt. The expedition was filled with many mishaps and disasters. After many long weeks of struggle, the team of explorers finally successfully mapped the entire river. Teddy almost died along the way. Due to the persistent help of his son, Kermit, Teddy made it. The Brazilian government honored Teddy by renaming the river the Rio Roosevelt, also called Rio Teodoro.

When Teddy returned home, he never quite regained his health. Although he was interested in writing and politics, the events of World War I distressed him. It was a terrible blow when his youngest son, Quentin, was killed while flying a fighter plane in 1918.

Teddy's face is carved into Mt. Rushmore, South Dakota.

Earth Heroes: Champions of the Wilderness

Teddy died in his sleep at his Sagamore Hill home on January 6, 1919. He is remembered as the president who brought the U.S. into the 20th century as a world leader. He believed it was the government's responsibility to have a positive influence on people both at home and abroad.

Teddy had big ideas and used forceful means to achieve his goals. He "busted trusts," used "gunboat diplomacy," "spoke softly and carried a big stick," started the "Bull Moose Party," and made possible the building of the Panama Canal. Teddy's face appears on Mount Rushmore along with Washington's, Lincoln's, and Jefferson's.

One of his most positive lasting contributions is the protection he provided to forests, prairies, mountains, rivers, animals, and natural resources. Millions of people benefit from his far-sighted actions every time they visit a national park, forest reserve, or wildlife refuge. Teddy encouraged many naturalists, urging them to write about their experiences as a way to educate and inspire others. He helped form the foundation of the environmental movement that continues today. When the National Wildlife Federation established the Conservation Hall of Fame in 1965, Theodore Roosevelt was given first place![12]

FAST FACTS

Born: October 27, 1858, New York, New York

Died: January 6, 1919, Oyster Bay, New York

First wife: Alice

Second Wife: Edith

Children: Alice, Theodore, Kermit, Archibald, Ethel, Quentin

ACCOMPLISHMENTS:
- Became twenty-sixth President of the United States
- Won Nobel Peace Prize
- Negotiated U.S. completion and control of the Panama Canal
- Wrote 26 books
- Established 21 reclamation projects, 150 national forests, 51 bird preserves, 4 game preserves, 5 national parks, and 18 national monuments
- Influenced conservation legislation including: The Reclamation Act and The Antiquities Act

RIPPLES OF INFLUENCE:

Famous People who Influenced Theodore Roosevelt:
Theodore Roosevelt (father), Gifford Pinchot, John Burroughs, John Muir, Henry Cabot Lodge

Famous People who Theodore Roosevelt Influenced:
John Hay, President Franklin D. Roosevelt, President Harry Truman, John McCain

TIMELINE OF IMPORTANT EVENTS

Theodore Roosevelt's Life		Historical Context
Born October 27	1858	
	1859	Darwin publishes *The Origin of Species*
	1861-1864	U. S. Civil War
	1862	Henry David Thoreau dies
Begins Roosevelt Museum of Natural History	1865	President Lincoln assassinated
	1867	Alfred Nobel patents dynamite
Learns taxidermy	1869	Suez Canal opens
Attends Harvard; marries Alice Lee	1876-1880	
	1876	Alexander Graham Bell invents telephone
	1879	Edison invents incandescent electric light
Serves as Assemblyman for New York	1882-1984	
First wife dies, goes to Dakota Territory	1884	
	1885	Louis Pasteur creates rabies vaccination
Marries Edith Carow	1886	
	1887	Aldo Leopold is born
Becomes Police Commissioner of NYC	1895	
Becomes Assistant Secretary of the Navy	1897	
Leads Rough Riders; becomes Gov. of NY	1898	
Becomes President	1901	
Establishes the first national parks	1902	Margaret Murie is born
Leases Panama Canal Zone	1903	Wright Brothers fly airplane
Serves second term as President	1904-1909	
Establishes National Forest Service	1905	
Receives Nobel Peace Prize	1906	The Great San Francisco Earthquake
Inventories of natural resources	1908	
Leads hunting expedition to Africa	1909-1910	
	1909	NAACP forms in New York City
	1910	British Empire covers 1/5 of world land area
Unsuccessfully runs for President	1912	
Explores Brazil's River of Doubt	1914	World War I begins; John Muir dies
Quentin, youngest son, dies in WWI	1918	Versailles Peace Treaty is signed
Dies January 6	1919	

Theodore Roosevelt

53

54 Earth Heroes: Champions of the Wilderness

Aldo Leopold
1887–1948

Father of Forest Wilderness Conservation

"Wilderness is a resource which can shrink but not grow."

Aldo Leopold spent his days as a young forester traveling on horseback through Arizona's backcountry. One afternoon, he and a member of his crew were eating their lunch on a rocky ledge overlooking the Blue River. They noticed an animal below. At first they thought it was a deer. Then six grown wolf pups sprang from under cover to playfully greet their mother. They realized their mistake. It was a wolf!

Hurriedly, Aldo and his companion grabbed their rifles. They fired into the pack "with more excitement than accuracy." Then they scrambled down to find the wolf. Unable to move, she glared defiantly at Aldo. He saw a "fierce green fire" in her eyes. Then she died.

Aldo never forgot that fierce green fire. Years later in one of his most famous essays, "Thinking Like a Mountain," he wrote, "I realized then, and have known ever since, that there was something new to me in those eyes—something known only to her and to the mountain. I was young then, and full of trigger-itch . . . ."[1]

Like most people of the time, Aldo thought that fewer wolves meant more deer. No one passed up an opportunity to kill a wolf. However, Aldo always kept an open mind to the lessons nature had to teach him. The look in the dying wolf's eyes was life-changing. It taught him that he needed to appreciate the importance of every part of an ecosystem, even predators like the wolf. And it helped him shape a new understanding about the complexity of the relationships among people, animals, and the land.

Aldo's nature lessons began early in his life. He was born in 1887 in Burlington, Iowa. The house he grew up in had an expansive view of the Mississippi River. He lived right next door to his grandparents, and enjoyed the freedom of running back and forth between two houses. His grandfather involved the whole family in many different gardening projects. At a very young age Aldo learned how to grow vegetables, plant flowers, and prune trees.

He and his grandfather spent many afternoons walking through the gardens together, inspecting all of the plants. Aldo loved to listen to his grandfather's stories. He also watched him sketch lively little pictures of the garden's birds, rabbits, and squirrels. These early experiences made a huge impression on him. Years later Aldo gave his own children similar experiences as they worked and played together on their Wisconsin farm.

The trees near Aldo's hilltop home were filled with birds. By the age of eleven Aldo had identified thirty-nine species. As a teenager he got up before dawn and used his grandmother's opera glasses to spy on the birds high up in the branches. He then faithfully recorded his observations in a notebook. His scientific approach towards nature lasted throughout his life. Even though he was young, Aldo had a high opinion of his skills and abilities. He didn't want to be called a mere "bird watcher;" he preferred "amateur ornithologist."

Observing birds did more than stimulate his intellect. It also opened his heart to the beauty he saw, and Aldo developed a deep, inner reverence for nature.

Aldo's father, Carl, nurtured his son's love of nature through many outings and hunting trips. Carl often left his gun at home as he guided family and friends into the woods just to "observe the goings-on." One of Aldo's friends was delighted by the interesting way Carl shared his knowledge. "He would open up a decaying hollow log to show us the life dwelling inside, such as mice or large insects. If we came to a certain type of old tree snag he would point out the signs that showed it to be occupied by mink . . . ."[2] Aldo adopted this style of "lecture on the move" later in his life with his college students.

Carl's views on hunting were ahead of their time. He realized that many species would be completely wiped out if hunters continued unlimited shooting of animals. So he developed his own personal code of sportsmanship and conservation. Carl didn't force his views on his son. But through his example, Aldo grew up understanding the importance of protecting animals from over-hunting.

A favorite summer destination for Aldo, his sister, and two brothers was a resort called the Les Cheneaux Club. It was located on Marquette Island in the northern-most part of Lake Huron, just off the coast of

Aldo using his grandmother's opera glasses to watch birds.

Aldo Leopold

Michigan's Upper Peninsula. For six weeks every year he hiked, camped, sailed, and fished. He felt just like Daniel Boone!

The island was the perfect size for exploring. Aldo drew detailed maps of the trails and shoreline, illustrating them with his artwork. It was a glorious time as he imagined the mysteries of the wilderness that awaited him just over the northern horizon. When fall came, the Leopold family would return to Iowa. But on the way home Aldo would already be dreaming about his next visit to Marquette Island.

In school, Aldo was shy around his classmates, especially girls. And although he was a good student, he preferred to spend his time with his family or out in nature. He especially liked the companionship of dogs and had an Irish terrier named Spud. His classmates nicknamed Aldo "Spuddo" because Spud was always by Aldo's side.

When Aldo was in high school he began to choose the values that would guide him through life. He collected quotations such as the following that were meaningful to him.

> To make the world within our reach somewhat better for our living and gladder for our speech.—John Greenleaf Whittier
>
> Tis only noble to be good . . . .— Alfred Lord Tennyson
>
> Today is a new day. Begin it well and serenely . . . .
> — Ralph Waldo Emerson

He combined the ideals of these great men with his family's attitudes. In this way Aldo determined for himself what was right and wrong—a personal code of ethics.

In 1904, when he was almost seventeen, he left Burlington High School to attend Lawrenceville School, a boarding school in New Jersey. Leaving home was a momentous event for Aldo and his family. Everyone was going to miss him, especially his mother Clara. She urged him to write to her as often as possible. Aldo kept his promise, sometimes writing as many as four or five letters a week. He told his mother all about the school and his classes. But mostly his letters were filled with tales about his "tramps" through the woods and fields. They were descriptions of his observations of the plants, animals, and birds.

> I went north, across the county, about seven miles, and then circled back toward the west. Here every farm has a timber lot, sometimes fifteen or twenty acres, and it is a fine country for birds . . . . Flickers and Blue Jays are beginning to increase in number as the weather grows warmer. Song Sparrows and Meadowlarks are singing constantly, while Robins and Fox Sparrow are just beginning to try a few notes . . . .[3]

Every day, rain or shine, Aldo spent an hour or more tramping around outside. Within his first month of arriving at Lawrenceville School, Aldo had drawn and labeled a map of a 10-mile area around the school. And within the first few months he had increased his list of bird sightings to 274 species.

Aldo's classmates at Lawrenceville had never known anyone quite like him. At first they thought he was rather strange. They called him "the naturalist." But over time they became curious about his adventures in the woods. Some eventually joined him on his tramps.

Aldo had his gun at school. He continued to hunt, but his thoughts about hunting were changing. He wrote to his mother, "I cannot imagine wanting to kill anything now when there is so much to see and appreciate out of doors."[4] In another letter he expressed his conservation ideas:

> I am very sorry that the ducks are being slaughtered as usual, but of course could expect nothing else. When my turn comes to have something to say and do against it and other related matters, I am sure that nothing in my power will be lacking to the good cause.[5]

Not only did he grow up to have a "say" about the environment, he so greatly influenced other peoples' thinking that he became known as the "father of wildlife ecology."

Aldo's habit of writing letters continued when he became a college student at Sheffield Scientific School at Yale University. However, the content of his letters changed. He began to write as much about people as he did about nature. And in addition to tramps in nature he also spent time going to dances. He was learning to be more social! His mother was very pleased that Aldo was overcoming his shyness.

Over time Aldo learned to find a balance between socializing with people and spending time alone in nature. He wrote that there were two things that appealed to him: "the relation of people to each other, and the relation of people to land."[5]

From the time Aldo left Burlington as a teenager, his ambition was to become a forester. Being a forester appealed to him because he would be able to make a living doing what he loved to do—tramping through the woods. Forestry was a brand new type of job just developing in the United States. And the best place to learn how to become a forester was Yale's Forest School.

The wealthy Pinchot family had started the school in 1900. Gifford Pinchot was determined to educate Americans about how to use their forests. He believed forests should be managed to provide the most resources (lumber, minerals, and water) for the most people. He wanted to use resources wisely—conserve them—so they would last for a long time.

When Aldo started school at Yale, Pinchot's philosophy greatly influenced him. At about the same time, Pinchot was also influencing President Theodore Roosevelt. In 1905, Roosevelt made Pinchot Chief of the U.S. Forest Service. Millions of acres of forests were under his control.

However, not everyone agreed with Pinchot. Some people, like John Muir, thought that forests should be protected from logging and other uses. They were called "preservationists" because they wanted to preserve the forests just as they were. Preservationists believed the best use for the forest was for hiking, camping, and personal enjoyment. They wanted the wilderness saved for future generations.

Aldo could see value in both perspectives. He wanted to use the country's natural resources wisely. In that way he was in agreement with conservationists like Pinchot. But he also wanted other people to enjoy the wilderness as he did. In that way he agreed with preservationists like Muir. Throughout his life Aldo struggled with these conflicting approaches. He tried to determine what it meant to protect the environment. He continuously examined his ideas and modified his thinking so that he could to do the "right" thing.

Aldo on his horse, Polly

When Aldo graduated from forestry school in 1909, he was hired by the U.S. Forest Service as a forest ranger in southeastern Arizona. His first big assignment was to map an area of the forest and estimate the amount of timber that could be harvested from it.

It was a physically difficult and mentally challenging job. Although Aldo was very experienced tramping in nature, he made many errors in his timber calculations. He also had difficulties managing his crew. But Aldo learned from his mistakes. In the years that followed, he earned the respect of both his crew and supervisor.

During the fifteen years he worked in the Southwest, Aldo observed the devastating effects that cattle grazing, wild fires, and soil erosion were having on the land and native animals. His observations led him to question some of the Forest Service's policies. One of his recommendations was for the government to protect some lands as wilderness areas. He felt passionately that wilderness "was not just a place to hunt, but a place to know the freedom of adventure, the joy of self-expression, and the value of self-restraint . . . The significance of wilderness was not merely recreational, but cultural."[6]

Many people were opposed to his wilderness proposal, but he continued to talk and write about it. Finally in 1924, 600,000 acres of the Gila National Forest in New Mexico were officially established by the Forest Service as the Gila Wilderness. This was the *first* designated wilderness area in the United States and all the world. It was a huge accomplishment!

While working in the Southwest, Aldo met Estella Bergere. She was the daughter of a prominent Spanish-Italian family in Sante Fe. He was immediately attracted to her, but his shyness prevented him from telling her how he felt. Then he heard that another man had proposed to Estella! Finally Aldo got up the courage to ask her to marry him. It took Estella several weeks to make up her mind. Finally she said, "Yes!" Aldo was the happiest he had ever been.

Throughout their thirty-six years of marriage, Estella supported Aldo in his work. She took on all of the responsibilities of managing their home and raising their five children. That gave Aldo the time he needed to pursue his career in nature.[7]

In 1924, Aldo and his family made a big change. They moved from New Mexico to Madison, Wisconsin. Aldo continued to work for the Forest Service, but he wasn't happy with his job. He decided to pursue his real interest—game management.

In his new job, Aldo surveyed game throughout several states and continued to develop his ideas about animals and their habitat. He taught hunters and farmers how to increase game populations by caring for the animals' natural habitats. Aldo came to see "the land" as a living community that included soil, water, plants, and animals. If the land was healthy, he believed all parts of it would be in balance, including wildlife.

As a professor at the University of Wisconsin, Aldo took his students out of the classroom and into the field. He taught them how to see nature

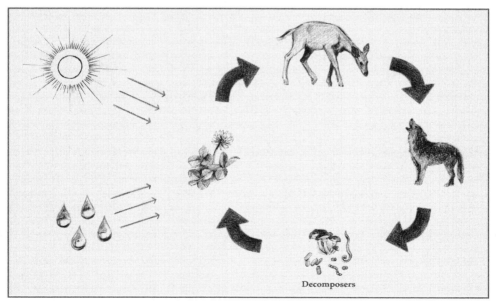

Aldo taught his students about food webs and that all parts of nature are connected.

in a new way. Game management wasn't just about animals. It was about the land as a whole. Unlike many scientists, he didn't separate nature into different subjects, like biology, zoology, forestry, and agriculture. Instead, he showed his students how all of the sciences were connected—just as everything on the land was connected.

Aldo's explanations of food chains, biotic pyramids, and the flow of energy throughout a land community were radical new concepts. He was teaching "ecology." Ecology is a word commonly used today, but in the 1930s few people had heard of it.

Scientists, hunters, and policymakers from around the country were interested in Aldo's thoughts and ideas. His reputation grew. Soon the university established a Department of Wildlife Management and made Aldo the first chairman.

Aldo was concerned about how quickly America's wilderness was vanishing. In 1935, he joined five other conservationists to create The Wilderness Society. The Society believed:

> A wilderness, in contrast with those areas where man and his own works dominate the landscape, is hereby recognized as an area where the earth and its community of life are untrammeled by man, where man himself is a visitor who does not remain.

It took many years, but in 1964 the Wilderness Act established the National Wilderness Preservation System. Nine million acres of land were set aside as wilderness. By 2008, there were over 107 million acres being protected in 704 Wilderness Areas throughout the United States.

Aldo put his environmental theories into practice when he bought a run-down farm on the Wisconsin River north of Madison. He dreamed of restoring the land to what it looked like before the white man took it away from the Indians.

As part of the restoration process Aldo, his family, friends, and students planted more than 40,000 pines and countless hardwood trees. They found native grasses growing along railroad tracks and in cemeteries

Aldo converted an old chicken coop into a simple retreat, "the Shack."

and replanted them in the worn-out soil. His daughter recalls, "From April to October, scarcely a weekend went by that someone did not plant or transplant something . . ."[8] Gradually the land responded, and today the farm is a beautiful, thriving prairie.

An old chicken coop—fondly called "the Shack"—became the family's weekend home. Their first task was to clean out years of accumulated chicken manure. Over the years, they worked together to build a fireplace, add a bunkhouse, put on a new roof, and drill a well. Aldo kept everything at the Shack very simple. He allowed only the bare essentials to be brought there. It was a refuge from what he called "too much modernity." He loved to get up before sunrise and sit outside with his coffee pot and journal, writing down his thoughts and feelings about the natural world around him.

Aldo, Estella, and their youngest daughter were at the Shack on April 24, 1948, when they saw smoke coming from their neighbor's land. They discovered it was a grass fire moving out of control. It was headed toward the stand of pines they had planted! Aldo immediately started fighting the fire, while Estella went for help. As Aldo was trying to beat down the flames, he suddenly had a heart attack and died.

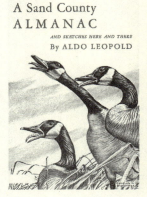

His death was totally unexpected. It shocked everyone, including many conservationists who looked to Aldo for inspiration. Just one week before he died, Aldo reached one of his most important goals: he found a publisher for a book he had been working on for many years. The book was called *A Sand County Almanac: And Sketches Here and There*. It begins, "There are some who can live without wild things, and some who cannot. These essays are the delights and dilemmas of one who cannot."

A Sand County Almanac is a combination of journal entries and essays. In an entertaining style, Aldo describes the sights and sounds of the seasons at the Shack. He imagines how a tiny chickadee survived five cold winters and relates the events that a huge oak tree witnessed before it fell. Some of his essays sound like poetry:

> The wind that makes music in November corn is in a hurry. The stalks hum, the loose husks whisk skyward in half-playful swirls, and the wind hurries on . . . So would I—if I were the wind.[9]

Throughout his life, Aldo lived by his own personal set of ethics—the values that helped him decide if something was right or wrong. In his essay "The Land Ethic" he states, "A thing is right when it tends to preserve the integrity, stability, and beauty of the biotic community. It is wrong when it tends otherwise."

Aldo influenced many others to think about what they considered right and wrong concerning the environment. He helped people see the natural world in a new way—in an interconnected way.

In 1980, the U.S. Forest Service honored Aldo and his wilderness ideals. They designated over 202,000 acres in New Mexico as the Aldo

Leopold Wilderness. It is located next to the Gila Wilderness, the area that Aldo worked hard to preserve sixty years earlier.

Aldo believed that people need a close personal connection to the land. "When we see land as a community to which we belong, we may begin to use it with love and respect."[10] The Leopold Foundation keeps Aldo's message alive by teaching classes and workshops. The farm and the Shack are open to the public, and many people visit throughout the year.

Another lasting legacy that Aldo left behind is the love for the land he gave to his children. All five of them became naturalists and have made significant contributions to the conservation movement. They are examples of the Leopold family's dedication to the well-being of the environment.

Aldo writing in front of the Shack with his dog

FAST FACTS

Born: January 11, 1887, Burlington, Iowa

Died: April 12, near Baraboo, Wisconsin

Wife: Estella

Children: Starker, Luna, Nina, Carl, and Estella

ACCOMPLISHMENTS:

- Wrote the proposal for the first wilderness area in the world.
- Wrote the first textbook on wildlife management, *Game Management*
- Helped found The Wilderness Society
- Helped make respect for the wilderness a national priority
- Developed the science of wildlife ecology and the practice of wildlife management
- Helped define the environmental movement through his essays in *A Sand County Almanac*
- Raised five children who all made contributions to the environment
- Trained hundreds of students as scientists to study and care for the land

RIPPLES OF INFLUENCE:

Famous People who Influenced Aldo Leopold
Henry David Thoreau, Ralph Waldo Emerson, John Muir, Frank Chapman, Theodore Roosevelt, Gifford Pinchot, numerous colleagues, including Olaus Murie. Other major influences were Carl Leopold, Aldo's father, and Charles Starker, Aldo's grandfather.

Famous People who Aldo Leopold Influenced
Numerous colleagues, including Olaus Murie, Jay "Ding" Darling, Benton MacKaye, Robert Marshall, P.S. Lovejoy, and Hans Albert Hochbaum

TIMELINE OF IMPORTANT EVENTS

Aldo Leopold's Life		Historical Context
Born January 11	1887	
	1889	Richard St. Barbe Baker is born
	1901	Theodore Roosevelt becomes President
	1901	Margaret Murie is born
	1903	Wright Brothers fly airplane
Leaves home for Lawrenceville School	1904	
Attends Yale Forest School	1906-1909	
	1906	The Great San Francisco Earthquake
Begins working as a forester in Arizona	1909	
Works as a forester in New Mexico	1911	
Marries Estella Bergere	1912	New Mexico becomes 47th state
	1914-1918	World War I
	1919	Theodore Roosevelt dies
Moves to Madison, Wisconsin	1924	First wilderness area is established.
Leaves Forest Service; makes game surveys	1928	
	1930	Worldwide depression begins
Writes *Game Management*	1933	
Founds Wilderness Society; buys the Shack	1935	
	1936	David Suzuki is born
	1937	Dow Chemical develops plastic
Heads Dept. of Wildlife Management	1939	World War II begins
	1940	Wangari Maathai is born
Begins writing ecological essays	1941	U.S. enters World War II
Dies April 21	1948	NATO is formed
A Sand County Almanac is published	1949	
	1980	Aldo Leopold Wilderness is designated

Richard St. Barbe Baker

1889–1982

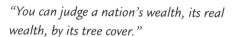

Man of the Trees

"You can judge a nation's wealth, its real wealth, by its tree cover."

The pine forest, dark and mysterious, tempted five-year-old Richard. He could hardly wait to explore it. At first he followed the path, but soon he found himself in a dense part of the forest. Then the path disappeared into a thick tangle of ferns. The ferns were taller than he was. As he walked underneath them, the sunlight shining through the fronds cast a green glow over his head.

The undergrowth was so thick he could only see a few yards ahead. But he wasn't afraid. He was exhilarated! The further he walked, the more joyful he became. The ferns gradually grew shorter and gave way to a clearing. Dry pine needles covered the forest floor like a soft, brown carpet.

It was here that young Richard had a mystical experience. He felt united with all of creation. There was no separation, only oneness. He was alone, but felt deeply connected to all of the living creatures he loved so dearly. He was lost, but felt only bliss. Overwhelmed with the beauty all around him, he sank to the ground.

In that moment his heart "brimmed over with a sense of unspeakable thankfulness"[1] that followed him through all of his life. He called it "his woodland rebirth" because it completely altered his outlook on life. When he returned home, everything was the same, yet different. The bread seemed sweeter, the big black dog friendlier, the grouchy gardener kinder, and his parents' love for him stronger. He couldn't understand it at the time, but looking back on the experience he realized that it helped him love life. At age 81 he wrote, "To me each day is more wonderful than the previous one...."[2]

Many wonderful days filled Richard St. Barbe Baker's long life. As an adult he was affectionately called by his middle name, St. Barbe—a French surname that had been in his family for generations. His admirers considered him a "saint" because he whole-heartedly devoted himself to helping the planet. He called himself a conservationist and an "Earth Healer."

His magical time in the pine forest wasn't the only nature experience that nurtured a deep love of trees in young St. Barbe. All of his earliest and happiest memories were connected to trees. As soon as he could walk, he toddled outside his house in the south of Hampshire, England, to sit in a sunny spot on the pine needles. When he was older, he climbed into the pine tree's branches. Sometimes the wind in the boughs sounded like music. At other times it sounded like waves breaking on the seashore. In his autobiography, *My Life, My Trees*, he wrote:

> Those pines spoke to me of distant lands and gave me my first desire to travel and see the trees of other countries. At times I would imagine that these tall pines were talking to each other as they shook or nodded their heads at whim of the winds.[3]

Growing a garden was another early childhood experience that influenced St. Barbe's life-long passion for planting trees. He had his first garden in 1891, when he was only two years old. He grew nasturtiums. His nanny helped him scratch the letters of his name in the soil, and he planted white mustard seeds along the lines. He was so proud when the little green sprouts came up and spelled his name: RICHARD.

His garden became a favorite place to play. When he was four, he bent flexible willow branches to make an archway for the garden's entrance. It was just high enough for him to walk under. He got quite a thrill when the arch sprouted leaves! He made a flagpole and placed it in the center of his garden. Each morning he hoisted a little flag to signal the start of the day, and each evening he lowered the flag and carefully rolled it up.

His father managed a tree nursery, and St. Barbe would watch him go about his work of growing trees. St. Barbe considered it a special treat to plant tree seeds in the long, narrow beds he helped prepare. He would rather plant trees than play cricket with the other boys. As the tree seedlings came up, St. Barbe thought they looked like regiments of soldiers. He "protected, weeded, and watered them. Their care was more important [to him] than any game."[4] While other boys played with toy soldiers, St. Barbe played with tree seedlings.

As St. Barbe grew older, he learned to graft buds onto the apple trees in his father's orchards. It took skill and patience to wrap the bud on to the tree trunk in the correct way. But even as a boy, his grafts were sometimes more successful than those of the professional gardeners.

Not only were trees his friends, they were also a source of comfort. Whenever St. Barbe was unhappy or upset about something that had happened during the day, he would run down to a special beech tree that grew in the woods near his home. Standing next to the friendly beech, he would imagine that he had roots digging down deep into Mother Earth and that all above he was sprouting branches. He would hold that image in his mind for a few moments, and soon he would feel the strength of the tree within himself. His heart would feel radiant. Then he would return with a fresh, positive perspective, at peace with whatever had happened.

When St. Barbe was twelve, he watched one of his neighbors at work with his beehives. The neighbor pulled out a frame covered with buzzing bees and handed it to St. Barbe. What a thrill! St. Barbe wanted a hive of his own. He traded some of the apple trees he had grafted for a

Richard St. Barbe Baker

beehive, and he was on his way to become a beekeeper. Within four years he had 16 hives producing honey—the best one yielding 240 pounds in one season.

His beekeeping skills were put to an especially good use when he was in college after World War I. Many of his classmates had lost arms, legs, or were otherwise injured in the war. They were extremely depressed. St. Barbe had the idea to start a beekeeping club to give them something meaningful to do. He bought all of the apiary equipment and found an orchard for the hives. He taught the basics of beekeeping to the eager club members, and at the end of the term they sold their honey. Then each member took home a hive for his own use. Establishing a beekeeping club is just one of many examples of the creative ways St. Barbe found to help others. He wanted everyone to enjoy life as much as he did.

At thirteen, St. Barbe went away to boarding school where he learned about the Canadian wilderness. The thought of wilderness adventures was so exciting! He wanted to go to Canada with all his heart. Finally, at the age of nineteen, he had his opportunity. His church was looking for missionaries to preach to the new settlers in Canada's western provinces, and he convinced his father he should go.

St. Barbe sailed across the Atlantic and rode across the Canadian prairie to get to Saskatchewan. Near the town of Saskatoon, he pitched a tent at Beaver Creek. He got up early each morning and saw the beavers busy building a dam. When St. Barbe returned in the winter to check on their progress, he could hardly believe his eyes. The beavers had turned a 12-foot wide stream into a 140-foot wide pond that flooded over 12 acres. Impressed with their natural skills, he came to regard them as "fellow foresters."[5]

In 1909, St. Barbe was one of the first 100 students to attend the University of Saskatchewan. Being self-reliant and independent, he found a variety of ways to pay for his classes. One of his moneymaking projects was trading wool blankets with the First Nations people (the Native Americans of Canada) in exchange for horses. St. Barbe built

Seeing the clear-cut forests in Canada influenced St. Barbe to become a forester.

a barn for his ponies on campus and earned a reputation as being an excellent horseman.

As he traveled by horseback across the wind-swept prairie, St. Barbe noticed "wide areas had been ploughed up where for centuries dwarf willows had stabilized the deep, rich, black soil."[6] Without the trees, there was nothing to protect the exposed topsoil from the wind. It blew away at a rate of one to four inches a year. St. Barbe called it a "desert in the making," and the sight of this tremendous waste shaped his life as a conservationist. During his three and half years in Canada, he encouraged farmers to plant trees as "shelter belts" around their homesteads and fields.

While working in a lumber camp in northern Saskatchewan, St. Barbe was shocked and deeply influenced by another scene of waste. The wilderness forests were heavily logged and a vast number of trees were left on the ground. It broke his heart to see such a loss. When he left for

England in 1912, he was determined that one day he would be a forester, protecting the trees and the environment.

Upon his return to England, he entered Cambridge University. However, World War I interrupted his education. Because of his expertise with horses, he became a trainer for the Horse and Field Artillery units and also helped transport horses across the English Channel to the front lines in France. Although it wasn't part of his assignment, St. Barbe went outside at night to spot the flashes from German guns as they were fired from behind their lines. The information he gathered was considered so valuable he was honored with the Military Cross. During the war he was badly wounded three times, once being left for dead on the battlefield. He said he owed his recovery to the skill of the doctors and devoted care of the nurses.

After the war ended he went back to school and graduated with a degree in forestry. His first job as a forester came in 1920 through the Colonial Office in Kenya, Africa, which at that time was a British colony.

St. Barbe was shocked to see the results of forest destruction in Kenya. The native trees, such as cedars and olives, were clear-cut. Then the forest was burned to make way for cash crops, such as tea and coffee. These were grown as single crops (monoculture) on large plantations. The soil became depleted of nutrients because it wasn't being naturally renewed by decaying leaves and vegetation. The forest lost its diversity, and the natural ecosystem was destroyed. Chemical fertilizer had to be used to grow the crops, causing further harm to the environment.

St. Barbe knew the only hope was to restore the forests with native trees. He set to work establishing tree nurseries. However, it was too big a project to do alone. He needed the help of the local tribesmen, the Kikuyu, to grow and plant thousands of tree seedlings. But the Kikuyu didn't have a tradition of planting trees. He had to find a way to encourage their cooperation.

He noticed that they had a special dance for many events—a dance when the beans were planted, a dance when the corn was harvested. He thought, "Why not a dance when the trees are planted? A Dance of the Trees!"[7] Working with the local chiefs, he announced that he was holding a dance. Over 3,000 Kikuyus came. St. Barbe chose many of these dancers to become his tree-planting volunteers. This group became known as *Watu wa Miti*, the Men of the Trees. To recognize one another they used the password *twahamwe*, which meant "all as one." Each volunteer made three promises: to protect the native forest, plant ten native trees each year, and take care of trees everywhere. These Kikuyu Men of the Trees established large nurseries on their land and raised over a million tree seedlings.

Years later, in the 1950s, much of Kenya was experiencing conflict. However, one area was peaceful. When the local Kikuyu chief was asked why this was so, he replied, "Over thirty years ago an English forester came. He taught us how to protect our native forest and plant native trees. We kept the promise we made to him over thirty years. We have had plenty of timber, plenty of fuel, plenty of water, plenty of food. No trouble!"[8] St. Barbe's volunteers had planted trees and harvested peace.

St. Barbe worked with the local people in Africa to plant trees.

More recently, another "champion of the wilderness," Wangari Maathai, has promoted peace in Kenya through treeplanting.

St. Barbe earned the affection of the Kikuyu tribesmen he trained because he deeply respected them. Many people in the British Colonial Office didn't. One day St. Barbe saw his superior officer about to hit one of the Kikuyu workers with the butt end of a riding crop. He immediately stepped in. The blow that was meant for the Kikuyu fell on St. Barbe, almost breaking his collarbone. The Kikuyu people never forgot this act of friendship. However, the Colonial Office was outraged that St. Barbe had defied authority. He was reassigned to Nigeria, far away from his Kikuyu friends.

His new Nigerian territory included a tropical rain forest, home to huge mahogany trees. Very little was known about rain forests in 1925, and St. Barbe was eager to study the forest canopy. However, the forest's undergrowth was tangled with so many vines, creepers, and interlacing leaves, he couldn't even see the tops of the tall trees. His solution was to make a ladder. He then climbed to the top of the tallest tree where he built an observation platform. From this treetop perch, he entered into a world unknown to those on the ground. He saw flowers, animals, and insects no person had ever seen. He wrote:

> I could look out on the whole dazzling life of the tree tops....How beautiful the whole scene was with tiny birds fluttering from flower to flower, butterflies camouflaged against their feathered enemies!...So little is known of the romantic life of the treetops where the dance of life goes on. Fertilization of flowers takes place, and seeds are formed and ripened in the sun's heat.[9]

Despite all of his forest innovations and successes, the Colonial Office never forgave him for protecting the Kikuyu worker. They fired him in 1929. At first this was a terrible disappointment for St. Barbe. He had worked so hard in the African forests. But he never regretted what he had done. And leaving his government job was the beginning of a new

St. Barbe studied the rain forest canopy from his tree-top platform.

life for St. Barbe. Later, he wrote: "My discharge from the Colonial Service liberated me for much greater work in reforestation and earth regeneration in other parts of the world."[10]

For over fifty years, St. Barbe traveled around the world spreading his message about the importance of the natural environment, especially trees. He became known as the Man of the Trees. He called trees the "Earth's skin," and explained that just as people needed skin to survive, the Earth needed trees to survive. He thought man had "rampaged over the stage of the earth, forgetting that he is only one of the players put there to play his part in harmony and oneness with all living things."[11] Whether he was in India or England, Africa or America, his message was the same: *plant trees to heal the Earth.*

St. Barbe identified the seven most important functions of trees: provide oxygen; play an essential role in the water cycle; aid food production by nurturing fertile soil; prevent soil erosion; maintain an ideal temperature for all forms of life; keep a balance of nature in the biodiversity of the forest ecosystem; provide timber.[12] He summed up the importance of trees in *Land of Tane*, one of the 30 books he wrote: "When the trees go, the rain goes, the climate deteriorates, the water table sinks, the land erodes, and desert conditions soon appear.[13]

St. Barbe not only shared his knowledge of forestry with people around the world, he also shared his inspiration. Dr. Alan Grainger wrote about St. Barbe's ability to inspire others with his enthusiasm: "Many foresters all over the world found their vocations as a result of hearing the Man of the Trees speak. I certainly did, but his impact is much wider than that. Through his global lecture tours, St. Barbe has made millions of people aware of the importance of forests to our planet."[14]

St. Barbe met with chiefs and presidents, tribesmen and children. He started Men of the Trees groups in 108 countries. Today the groups in England and Western Australia remain the most active.

Men of the Trees in England began when St. Barbe briefly returned home from Kenya in 1924. It is now called the International Tree Foundation. Like St. Barbe, they believe that planting a tree is an act of faith in the future—knowing that others not yet born will enjoy the benefits it brings. They work to make the world a better place now, and for generations to come, by planting, protecting, and promoting trees. His Royal Highness the Prince of Wales is the patron of the organization. In 1978, England gave St. Barbe one of the country's highest honors. He was made an officer in the Order of the British Empire (O.B.E.).

Men of the Trees began in Western Australia in 1979. With women now making up over half of its membership, the group runs a variety of community programs including the Children's Forest. This project gives parents, grandparents, and family friends the opportunity to mark the birth of a child by planting a tree. The Children's Forest creates a bond between children and trees, and it fulfills one of St. Barbe's dreams. As he said, "I have a dream of the whole Earth made green again. An Earth healed and made whole through the efforts of children of all ages and all nations planting trees to express their special understanding of the earth as their home."[15]

St. Barbe is especially remembered for two of his major undertakings: his work to save the redwood trees in California and his plans to reclaim millions of acres of the Sahara Deert.

He first saw the coast redwood trees in 1930. These redwoods are the tallest trees in the world, some as tall as a 35-story building and over 2,000 years old. St. Barbe was captivated by their age, height, and beauty. He called them "wonder trees." The California Save the Redwood League was trying to save individual trees or small groves. But St. Barbe wanted to save a much larger area—at least 12,000 acres—to sustain the micro-climate that the trees needed to survive.

In search of an appropriate grove, he traveled northward along the California coast. One night he camped inside a hollow redwood tree. When he found broken arrowheads right next to the tree, he was pleased to think that Native Americans had camped in that same spot centuries

California redwoods are the tallest trees in the world.

Richard St. Barbe Baker

before. At Mill Creek near Crescent City, he found trees that represented "the supreme achievement of tree growth" in the world. This was the place he was looking for! He would call it the Grove of Understanding.

Protecting the redwoods became his top priority, and when he returned to England he set up a nation-wide tour. As the English people heard about the magnificent trees, they generously contributed to his "Save the Redwoods Fund." When Americans learned that the English were trying to save *their* trees, they also started making donations. St. Barbe returned to the U.S. every spring to spread his message about saving the trees. Finally, in 1939, he achieved his goal! Twelve thousand acres of redwoods were handed over to the state of California to be preserved for all time. This area is now part of Redwood National Park.

In 1952, St. Barbe led a 9,000-mile expedition to survey the Sahara Desert. He was alarmed at the rate that the desert was advancing. He proposed planting a "Green Front" of trees to stop the desert from spreading. After a 25,000-mile expedition in 1964, he specifically outlined his ideas for reclaiming the desert through tree planting. Twenty-four countries supported his plan. But due to political differences among the nations involved, his monumental goal has not yet been achieved. The reclamation of the Sahara Desert remains an environmental concern addressed by the United Nations.

St. Barbe's life overflowed with creativity, enthusiasm, and vitality. He wrote 30 books, rode the length of New Zealand (over 900 miles) on horseback when he was seventy-four years old, studied Chinese while in his 80s, and planted trees his entire life. He planted his last tree on the campus of the University of Saskatoon just four days before he died at the age of ninety-three.

Many of his ideas and projects that seemed outlandish when they were first proposed had become widely appreciated by the time of his death. He was well ahead of his time in advocating sustainable forestry and desert reclamation. He also correctly predicted the global impacts of deforestation. Today, he is recognized as one of the first pioneers of the global environmental movement.[16]

Peter Caddy of the Findhorn Community in Scotland paid tribute to St. Barbe saying: "If one man can do so much, what couldn't we achieve if all of us worked together?" This was St. Barbe's hope. He wanted his life-long example of planting trees to encourage many others to dedicate their lives to the service of the Earth. And his hope was achieved. Over 26 trillion trees have been planted worldwide by the organizations St. Barbe started and those he influenced.

Throughout his life, St. Barbe remained dedicated to his vision of everyone working together in a world of wellbeing:

> I picture village communities of the future living in valleys protected by sheltering trees on the high ground. They will have fruit and nut orchards and live free from disease and enjoy leisure, liberty and justice for all, living with a sense of their oneness with the Earth and with all living things.

Children of the Green Earth in Seattle, Washington, is one of the many organizations created as a result of St. Barbe's inspiration. His spirit is reflected in the song the children sing when they plant trees:

St. Barbe dedicated his life to planting trees.

> *From our hearts*
> *With our hands*
> *For the Earth*
> *All the world together*[17]

Richard St. Barbe Baker   83

FAST FACTS

Born: October 9, 1889, near West End, Southampton, Hampshire, England

Died: June 9, 1982, Saskatoon, Saskatchewan, Canada

Wife: Doreen Long (first); Catriona Burnett (second)

Children: Angela, Paul

ACCOMPLISHMENTS

- Responsible for the planting of 26 trillion trees
- Began the Men of the Trees organization
- Pioneered the practice of social forestry, using local people to reforest their land
- Pioneered the global environmental movement
- Worked for environmental sustainability and desert reclamation
- Bestowed with the honor of Officer of the Order of the British Empire
- Helped save 12 thousand acres of California redwoods
- Wrote 30 books

RIPPLES OF INFLUENCE:

Famous People Who Influenced Richard St. Barbe Baker
Ralph Waldo Emerson, John Masefield, Henry Van Dyke, Alfred Lord Tennyson, Lord Baden Powell, radio broadcaster Lowell Thomas

Famous People Influenced by Richard St. Barbe Baker
President Franklin D. Roosevelt, Wangari Maathai, Prime Minister of India Nehru, Jomo Kenyatta, Shoghi Effendi of the Baha'i Cause, Peter Caddy, George Bernard Shaw, Sir Francis Younghusband

TIMELINE

Richard St. Barbe Baker's Life		Historical Context
	1887	Aldo Leopold born
Born October 9	1889	
Grows his first garden	1891	
Has a mystical nature experience	1894	
Becomes a beekeeper	1901	Roosevelt becomes Pres.; Margaret Murie born
	1903	Wright Brothers fly airplane
	1906	The Great San Francisco Earthquake
Enrolls in University of Saskatchewan	1909	
Sees "desert in the making" in Canada	1910	
Enters Cambridge	1912	New Mexico becomes 47th state
Serves in military	1914-1918	World War I
Helps establish the Ministry of Health	1919	Theodore Roosevelt dies
Begins Men of the Trees in Kenya	1922	
	1924	Wilderness Act is established
Works as forester in Nigeria and West Coast	1924-1929	
Establishes 40 nurseries in Palestine	1929	
Begins Save the Redwoods Fund	1930	Worldwide depression begins
	1936	David Suzuki is born
	1937	Dow Chemical develops plastic
Saves 12 thousand acres of redwoods	1939	World War II begins
	1940	Wangari Maathai is born
	1941	U.S. enters World War II
Establishes Forestry Assoc. of Great Britain	1946	
	1950s	Kenyans rebel against English
Leads first Sahara Desert expedition	1952	
Travels to New Zealand	1954	
Completes the Cobbett Ride in England	1958	
Rides the length of New Zealand	1963	Pres. Kennedy assassinated
Launches the Sahara Reclamation Programme	1964	Kenya becomes an independent country
Receives O.B.E.	1978	
Begins Men of the Trees in Australia	1979	
	1980	Aldo Leopold Wilderness is designated
Dies June 9	1982	

Margaret Murie

1902–2003

Grandmother of the Conservation Movement

"Alaska is the last treasure of wilderness that we'll ever have. I think we need to be very careful about what we do with it."

Mardy Murie's granddaughter, Robin, was struggling to make an important decision and wanted her grandmother's advice. Should she take a job in California? Robin presented all of the reasons, all of the pros and cons, as she tried to make up her mind. Mardy listened patiently, then simply said, "I'd always go for the adventure."[1]

Going for adventure is just what Mardy did her whole life—all 101 years of it! Adventure began in 1911 when she came to breakfast one fall morning. She found her mother reading a telegram from her stepfather. He had moved to Fairbanks, Alaska, and Mardy and her mother had been anxiously waiting to hear from him.

"Can you catch the Steamer Jefferson on September 15?" the telegram read. "Last steamer to connect with last boat down the Yukon. Will meet you in Dawson." They had to get to Dawson before the winter "freeze-up!" In a flurry of activity, Mardy and her mother packed their trunks and said hurried goodbyes to Seattle.

The days aboard ship flew by as Mardy explored her stateroom, raced around the deck, and listened to stories about Alaska from the other passengers. For nine-year-old Mardy, it was better than a big birthday party! When the steamship docked in Skagway, her journey continued by train, then by riverboat, and finally by horse-drawn cart far into the heart of northern Alaska.

Alaska was still a frontier. It wouldn't become a state for another half century. And Fairbanks was especially isolated. Located along the Chena River, it was four hundred miles from the coast and only a hundred miles from the Arctic Circle. The closest town was eight days away by horse sleigh or ten days away by river steamer. Mardy's mother thought, "It was as though a great clock somewhere had exploded, and one little cogwheel had been flung though space, landed in the arctic tundra, and continued spinning."[2]

Fairbanks was a bustling Gold Rush town of 5,000 people. There were five saloons for every church—a town built to suit a rough crowd of prospectors and loggers. To Mardy, Fairbanks was a happy-go-lucky place big enough for the wide assortment of people who came from all over the world to make their fortunes. There were Swedes, Serbs, Russians, Irishmen, and many others. They all had different languages, customs, and morals. Mardy loved the unusual conglomeration!

An atmosphere of tolerance and love filled the town. People relied on one another. To survive in the wilderness, they had to. Growing up in the midst of such diversity helped Mardy learn an important lesson: not to judge people by their outer appearance, but by their inner character.

Mardy's family lived in the last house on the last street on the edge of Fairbanks. Like many houses, it was a simple, four-room log cabin. Fabric was hung over the log walls and across the ceiling. Mardy's mother attached wallpaper to the fabric to create a homey feeling. Huge piles of wood filled the shed, and keeping the fire burning in the woodstove was a daily chore. Mardy's house eventually gained some modern conveniences such as electric lights and a telephone, but there was no running water—that was supplied by Fred the Waterman who arrived each day on his wagon or sleigh.

Mardy had a natural curiosity, and she kept her eyes open to all of the happenings in her wilderness environment. Each season brought new and memorable experiences. Winter, the longest season, lasted six months from October to April. Most days it was extremely dark and cold. "Daytime" in December consisted of only four hours of feeble light, followed by twenty long hours of darkness. And the temperatures sometimes dropped to -50° F., or 82 degrees below freezing. It was agony for Mardy to crawl out of bed in the morning! But in Alaska, life went on. So Mardy bundled up in her warmest parka and walked the half mile to school.

On weekends, her parents gave her freedom to roam around town. She and her husky, Major, pulled a little coaster sled as she explored the streets with other kids.

The snow-covered Valdez Trail was the town's only lifeline to the rest of the world, and life revolved around the weekly arrival of the mail sleigh. On mail day, children as well as adults crowded along Fairbanks's main street to wait for news from "the Outside," as well as supplies. Mardy would anxiously gather with her friends in the dim afternoon light, watching and listening. Then a cry would go up: "I hear the bells!" She would strain her ears to hear the tinkling. A shout of "I see 'em! Here they come!" would be followed by yells to the driver as he triumphantly pulled into town. To lonely prospectors, the sleigh meant letters from home. To Mardy, the sleigh meant special treats—fresh eggs, or oranges, or apples.

With spring came longer, warmer days. In April, the melting snow made the hill outside of town perfect for sledding. Mardy and her friends played outside for hours in the long evening twilight.

April was also the month when the ice broke up on the river. Mardy would be sitting in school listening to the drip, drip of water running off the roof, when suddenly she would hear the shriek of the fire siren followed by several short blasts of the town whistle—the signal that the "ice was going." She and her classmates would throw their books into

Margaret Murie

their desks and pour out of the school as the whole town rushed to the river. What a spectacle! Giant pans of ice were raised up on edge, carried along for a short distance, and then thrown down on other pans of ice, causing a huge pile-up.

Summer—"glorious summer," as Mardy called it—was the shortest season. Thankfully it had the longest days: 24 hours of daylight in June. Mardy's activities were almost as endless as the days were long. She picnicked with friends, played ball and tennis, picked flowers, explored the woods, and rode her bike. Most of all she picked berries. Mardy wrote, "Nature made it impossible for fruit trees to grow in the North. But she compensated for this with the most lavish gift of berries...."[3] Fresh fruit from the States was "more costly than jewels," and everyone in Fairbanks, from the oldest adult to the youngest toddler, would wander out onto the tundra to fill their buckets.

But there was one drawback: mosquitoes! Massive swarms of them filled the air. Mardy would smear herself with citronella, an insect

Mardy grew up in this log house on the edge of Fairbanks.

repellant, or wear a hat with a head net. Despite the constant nuisance of the bugs, summer always went by too fast.

At fifteen, Mardy's adventures took another turn. Her father unexpectedly came back into her life. Mardy's mother and her father, Ashton Thomas, had divorced when Mardy was five years old. Her beloved stepfather was the only father she really knew. But Ashton had contacted Mardy's mother, and it was decided that Mardy would spend the summer working at his fish canning company. That sounded like another adventure! Yet Mardy was hesitant about reuniting with her father. "Don't worry," her mother said reassuringly. "Meeting your father will be like a big warm breeze carrying you away." [4]

Mardy's destination was Port Ashton, a town named after her father. In order to get there, she had to travel the dangerous Valdez Trail. In 1918, it was extremely unusual for a young girl to travel alone. For a girl to take the Valdez Trail was completely unheard of. Nevertheless, Mardy was eager and determined to make the 375-mile trip. But as she packed her suitcase, she began to doubt herself. She wondered if she knew enough about how to get along in the world. "Aren't there any things you should tell me before I go?" she asked her mother.

"No," her mother sweetly responded. "You're going on sixteen. If I haven't raised you properly so far, there isn't much use trying to start now. I'm relying on your good sense."[5] Mardy's good sense successfully carried her through this adventure and many others in her life.

Melting snow made travel treacherous in the spring, and the horse-drawn sleigh needed to travel at night when the snow was cold and firm. So, tucked under a warm wolf-skin blanket, Mardy began her nine-day trip at midnight. As the town disappeared from her view, "the panicky emptiness" she felt inside of herself "fought against the enormous thrill of unimaginable adventure."

The sleigh driver, Roy, stayed awake by telling stories. Mardy wrote, "His talk opened a new world to me—the world of the trail—my imagination followed his words through blizzards and overflows and hurricane winds, injured horses, sick or insane passengers, murderers in the custody of deputy marshals, broken bridges, and fires in roadhouses—there was no end to the drama . . . on the Valdez Trail."[6]

Not only was the trip special for Mardy, it was also a momentous event for the entire town. A railroad was being built from Seward to Fairbanks, making reliance on horse-drawn sleighs obsolete. Mardy's trip was the final one for the company that brought sleighs in and out of Fairbanks. All along the trail the drivers and men at the roadhouses said their last goodbyes to one another. Mardy's trip marked the end of their way of life. This wouldn't be the last time that a significant event in history would be connected to a personal event in Mardy's life.

When Mardy arrived in Port Ashton, "she was greeted warmly by the members of her extended family—father, stepmother, uncles, cousins, and half-brother—and she was immediately plunged into the hectic and olfactory world of an Alaska fisheries business." [7] Her stepmother taught her to row a boat and together they explored the bays and inlets of Prince William Sound. She had many questions, and eagerly learned about tides and storms, fish and whales. Her father encouraged her, saying, "Curiosity, that divine thing, curiosity. It will carry you on when all else fails."[8]

After an action-filled summer, Mardy returned to Fairbanks to finish school. Most girls at that time ended their education with high school graduation, but not Mardy. She wanted to go to college. She chose Reed College in Portland, Oregon, which meant more long and adventure-filled trips. Although inspired by the professors who encouraged her independent thinking, she felt too shy to make many friends or participate in social events.

Mardy decided to try another school. She left Reed College to attend Simmons College in Boston. Her father was in Boston on business, and she stayed with him for a short while. However, the young women at that school didn't understand Mardy or her unique background. They called her "that girl from Alaska." So Mardy left Boston at the end of the school year and returned to Fairbanks.

Although she was uncertain about finishing college, it felt wonderful to be back in Alaska. She jumped into an active social life, joining her friends on picnics, hikes and outings. Her favorite activity was dancing, and she practiced all the latest dance steps at the weekly community dance. During a whirlwind of outdoor activities and parties, Mardy became reacquainted with a young man she had met the year before, Olaus Murie.

Olaus was in Fairbanks getting ready for a winter-long dogsled trip into the wilderness of the Brooks Range of northeast Alaska. He worked for the U.S. Bureau of Biological Survey (now the U.S. Fish and Wildlife Service), a government agency that studied and managed wildlife. As a field biologist, he researched animals in their natural habitat. He was on assignment to gather information about the great caribou herds.

Caribou lived in remote, unexplored areas, and very little was known about their feeding, mating, and migratory patterns. Olaus had already spent the previous winter observing them. He had collected specimens of their hooves, hides, and bones. When he met Mardy, he was preparing to continue his study.

Olaus was thirteen years older than Mardy. Calm and reserved, he didn't make much of an impression on her at first. But over time she came to realize how special he was. Describing a boating trip with Olaus, she wrote:

> At one place in the quiet water of Moose Creek we heard a great-horned owl hoot far off in the forest. Olaus answered him. Again the owl spoke, a bit closer this time. Olaus hooted again, and so it went, until suddenly out of nowhere, the dark soft shape floated into a treetop right above us and sat silhouetted against the golden sky. What kind of magic did this man have? And when we made camp later that evening he took out his notebook and made me a sketch of that owl. So he was an artist too?[9]

Yes, Olaus was an excellent artist. His field journals were filled with sketches and paintings of birds and animals. He had many other talents too. He was an expert on animal tracks. His book of drawings and descriptions is still used by biologists today. He also earned the well-deserved reputation of being one of the best travelers through the Alaskan wilderness, "for no one was more tireless, both physically and mentally."[10]

His outstanding skills of observation were recognized by George Schaller, an internationally known scientist, who wrote that Olaus "could discover more in an acre than most of us see in many square miles."[11] Because Olaus believed that the most valuable quality a scientist could have was his integrity, his reports were thorough and accurate.

Even though his work kept him busy conducting wildlife studies in the backcountry or writing up reports in Washington, D.C., Olaus and Mardy stayed in touch. Their friendship grew and deepened as they expressed their thoughts and feelings through long letters. When Olaus was camped at Mount McKinley National Park, now called Denali, Mardy made a rare visit. Later she wrote, "At the end of five days of tramping about in a rosey haze of those enchanted mountains, we both knew that there was no other life for us except together."[12]

They became engaged, but Olaus' work kept them apart for yet another year. Mardy made the most of the time by finishing her college education at the Alaska Agricultural College and School of Mines in Fairbanks, now called the University of Alaska. She made history as the only senior in the class of 1924 and the very first woman to graduate from the college.

Finally, after months of being separated, Mardy and Olaus traveled by different boats to a tiny log church on the banks of the Yukon River and were married on August 19, 1924. It was one day after Mardy's 22nd birthday.

Their honeymoon, a dogsled expedition into the wilderness, established the pattern of adventure for their married life. Mardy's field biology lessons began on their first day of marriage when Olaus taught her how to

Mardy and Olaus dressed in furs for their long honeymon expedition.

trap mice, collect plants, and identify birds. She wrote, "Even that first day I began to feel the magnetic charm of birds, of knowing them."[13]

Mardy was eager to become Olaus' field assistant. His knowledge and skill were a perfect match to her curiosity and enthusiasm. He opened her eyes to the rich life of the Alaskan wilderness. At first Mardy wondered if she would be a capable partner for Olaus, but he always had complete faith in her ability to learn whatever was necessary. She later wrote, "My husbad thought I could do anything—and he expected me to do it!" And she did.

From August through November, Mardy and Olaus explored the Brooks Range along the Koyukuk River. Mardy was often thrilled by her new adventures and experiences:

> An ideal day to hit the trail: twelve below, just right for mushing. We were both running and I was soon too warm; I threw back the parka hood . . . the crisp air felt good on my bared head. How light my

moccasined feet felt, padding along on snow-sprinkled ice at a dogtrot, exhilaration in every muscle responding to the joy of motion, running, running, without getting out of breath.[14]

At other times she acknowledged the hardships. After a difficult day of travel she wrote in her diary:

> I was kept at a steady trot behind [the sled], hanging on to the handle-bars, trying to hop over each obstacle as it appeared . . . I could not see them all quickly enough to dodge them, and occasionally my moccasin would get caught underneath one. This kept up until my toes felt skinned, cut, and bleeding, if not broken. Tears seemed near the surface . . . .[15]

At one point in the trip Olaus left on a two-day caribou hunt across the river while Mardy stayed behind to keep the fire going, to dry the caribou hides they had already collected. She wrote:

> Imagine an eight-by-ten tent occupied by three caribou hides, including hoofs, various camp equipment, one girl, no reading matter, and you have the picture. I was learning a bit more about being married to a scientist.[16]

When Olaus hadn't returned at dusk of the second day, Mardy started to worry—not for herself, as she felt at home in the wilderness, but for Olaus. She was sure something terrible had happened. Should she go look for him? Long past dark he arrived back at the tent. Mardy had had many hours to imagine the worst. She was in tears. Olaus comforted her and soon she was laughing.

However, Mardy wasn't at peace with herself. The next day she sat on a mountainside reflecting on the experience and had an important insight. She realized that she needed to change her thinking. She resolved to stay in control of her thoughts, put aside all worry, learn to trust, and wait serenely.

Mardy stands with a sled dog in front of the small tent she and Olaus used on their honeymoon expedition.

During the many challenges Mardy and Olaus faced on their honeymoon expedition, Mardy never failed to notice the magnificence of the wilderness landscape. The following descriptions from her book *Two in the Far North* paint a picture of some of Alaska's many moods:

> Even through fatigue and the ache of bruises, I felt its beauty. It was the North as it so often is, gray, quiet, self-sufficient, and aloof. You couldn't help feeling the strength of the land . . . [17] The sun was climbing higher, glowing through the purple willow branches, and gilding the yellow grasses of occasional sloughs. Every few minutes our winding trail gave us a glorious vista of white peaks . . . .[18] Spruce trees, black in shadow and emerald in the light, willows full of purple shades and alive with gossiping redpolls.[19]

After the trip, Mardy and Olaus spent the rest of the winter in Washington, D.C., where Olaus wrote up his reports for the Biological Survey. In the spring, Olaus left for an assignment on the Alaskan

Martin sits atop a mammoth tusk that Olaus and Mardy found on the Old Crow River expedition.

Peninsula. Mardy didn't go; she was expecting their first child. Martin was born on July 10, 1926.

When it came time for Olaus to go on his next expedition—banding geese on the Old Crow River in the Brooks Range—Mardy was not to be left behind. She and Martin would go, too! Friends and colleagues warned them that it was too dangerous to take a baby on a wilderness trip. Mardy and Olaus didn't listen to them. Little Martin fit snugly into a wooden box that was securely tied to the top of their boat.

Over the next several years Joanne and Donald were born. Mardy and all three children went with Olaus wherever his fieldwork took him. The children "grew and were brown and never had a sick moment. . . . They were busy from morning 'til night with places and objects they found right in the wilderness."[20]

In 1927, Olaus and Mardy moved to Jackson Hole, Wyoming, where Olaus was sent to study the largest elk herd in the U.S. outside of Alaska. The elk were mysteriously dying, and the government hoped that Olaus would be able to discover why.

After several years gathering scientific data, Olaus concluded that the elk were dying at a rapid rate because humans were disturbing the delicate balance of their wilderness ecosystem. Cattle ranches had taken over a lot of the elk's feeding area, and the elk were forced to eat rough vegetation that caused a deadly mouth disease. The ecosystem was further upset because the ranchers were killing wolves and mountain lions, which were the elk's natural predators. Olaus recommended that the government enlarge the size of the Elk Wildlife Refuge. Today the refuge covers nearly 25,000 acres of land and provides a winter home for 5,000 to 8,000 elk.

Olaus and Mardy continued to live in Jackson Hole even after the elk study was complete. The area reminded Mardy of her beloved Alaska.

A major turning point in their lives came in 1945 when Olaus resigned from the Biological Survey to become the Director of the Wilderness Society. Mardy said that their lives blossomed as they connected with so many people through the Society who felt the same way they did about saving the wilderness.

At this same time, they bought a beautiful piece of property in the Jackson Hole area—a former ranch, in a town called Moose. With the ranch as their home base, they devoted their full energies to wilderness preservation and conservation. Many Wilderness Society meetings were held at their ranch, and conservationists from around the country came to visit them. Always the gracious host, Mardy kept the cookie jar full as she welcomed all of their visitors and discussed ways to preserve wild places and animals.

In the 1950s Alaska once again became the focus of their attention. Starker Leopold, Aldo's son, and a few other prominent conservationists wanted to designate an area of northeast Alaska as a wilderness area. They asked Olaus and Mardy for help. Happily, they returned to the Brooks Range—to investigate the Sheenjek Valley. Mardy's heart soared as she and Olaus made their camp in the pristine wilderness.

One afternoon, after hiking towards the top of a mountain, Mardy said that she knew what John Muir meant when he said, "Go climb the mountains and get their good tidings." She didn't just feel glad, she felt perfectly contented.

After leaving the Sheenjek, Olaus and Mardy did all they could to educate people about the importance of preserving the Arctic. Finally in

December of 1960, after years of struggle, a telegram arrived for Olaus and Mardy at the local post office. (They didn't have a phone at the ranch). An Executive Order by the Secretary of the Interior had established the Arctic National Wildlife Range! Mardy and Olaus hugged and wept with relief and joy.

In addition to fighting for environmental causes, Olaus had also been fighting against cancer and other diseases for years. In 1963 he died at the age of seventy-four. A part of Mardy died too. Their lives had been so deeply intertwined through their love of nature and their love for each other. John Denver commemorated their special relationship in his lyrics for "A Song for Two Lovers":

> I see them dancing somewhere in the moonlight,
> Somewhere in Alaska, somewhere in the sun.
> I hear them singing a song for all lovers,
> A song for the two hearts beating only as one.

Mardy had lost Olaus, but she had not lost her passion for the land. She continued working for The Wilderness Society as well as helping other environmental organizations such as the Sierra Club. She was invited to the White House for the signing of the Wilderness Act, a law that created the Wilderness Preservation System. What a victory for the wilderness! Mardy believed that people needed wilderness for five reasons: space, research, watershed protection, recreation, and spiritual renewal.[21]

The more Mardy spoke before audiences, the more confident she became. As Alaskan environmentalist Celia Hunter commented, "She simply said yes to the opportunities that came her way to express her feelings, to stand up for wilderness wherever it was threatened, and it grew on her, and it was very becoming."[22] When a controversy arose over the value of wilderness preservation, Mardy would be contacted, and she willingly gave her voice to the cause.

She returned to Alaska to survey wilderness areas for the National Park Service. She also worked on the Alaska National Interest Lands

Conservation Act that became law in 1980. It is often called the most significant land conservation measure in the history of our nation. It protected over 100 million acres of federal lands in Alaska, doubling the size of the country's national park and refuge system and tripling the amount of land designated as wilderness.

Mardy never sought recognition, yet she received every major environmental award, including the Audubon Medal, the John Muir Award, and the Robert Marshall Conservation Award. She was made an Honorary Park Ranger and received an honorary Ph.D. from the University of Alaska. In 1998, President Clinton awarded her the Presidential Medal of Freedom. He said, "We owe much to the life's work of Mardy Murie, a pioneer of the environmental movement, who, with her husband, Olaus, helped set the course of American conservation . . . "

Mardy dedicated the last part of her life to teaching young people. Even when she was well into her 90s Mardy held classes at her home. She said, "I've had enough experiences for twelve lifetimes. So I feel that the least I can do is to try to save what little we have left for the future. I know a lot of young people will appreciate this country if given a chance. But they can't if the country isn't there." [23]

Mardy wanted to ensure that the conservation work that was so important to her and Olaus continued after she was gone. With the help of the Teton Science Schools, her home and property in Moose was established as the Murie Center—a place for people to experience nature and learn about the importance of conservation. Mardy died at her home on October 19, 2003, at the age of 101.

Robert Redford, actor, producer, and environmentalist said of Mardy, "Generations to come will feel her imprint, though they may not know it was how she lived her life that allowed them to witness some of the last wild places on Earth."

FAST FACTS

Born: August 18, 1902, Seattle, Washington
Died: October 19, 2003, Moose, Wyoming
Husband: Olaus
Children: Martin, Joanne, and Donald

ACCOMPLISHMENTS:
- Helped bring about the passage of the Alaska National Interest Lands Conservation Act, the greatest land preservation act in U.S. history
- Helped create the Arctic National Wildlife Refuge
- Received many awards, including the Audubon Medal, the John Muir Award, Robert Marshall Conservation Award, and the J.N. Ding Darling Conservationist of the Year Award (the National Wildlife Federation's highest honor)
- Received the Presidential Medal of Freedom, the highest civilian honor awarded by the United States.
- Wrote three books, *Two in the Far North*, *Wapati Wilderness*, and *Island Between*
- Campaigned to enlarge the boundaries of the Olympic National Park and to create the Jackson Hole National Monument

RIPPLES OF INFLUENCE:

Famous People who Influenced Mardy and Olaus
Many associates in the conservation movement, including Aldo Leopold, Adolph Murie (brother), Benton MacKaye, Robert Marshall, Howard Zahniser

Famous People who Mardy and Olaus Influenced:
Supreme Court Justice William O. Douglas, President Dwight D. Eisenhower, John Denver, Terry Tempest Williams, George Schaller, and associates in the conservation movement mentioned above

TIMELINE

Margaret Murie's Life		Historical Context
Olaus Murie, husband, born March 1	1889	Richard St. Barbe Baker is born
	1901	Roosevelt creates first wildlife refuge
Born August 18	1902	
	1905	Audubon Society is formed
	1906	Antiquities Act is passed
Moves to Fairbanks	1911	
	1913	Muir loses battle for Hetch Hetchy Valley
Olaus goes to Arctic for first time	1914	W.W. I begins
	1919	Theodore Roosevelt dies
Meets Olaus	1921	
Graduates college; marries Olaus Murie	1924	Wilderness Act established
Martin is born	1925	
Moves to Jackson Hole, Wyoming	1926	
Joanne is born	1927	
	1930	Worldwide depression begins
Donald is born	1931	
	1935	The Wilderness Society is created
	1936	David Suzuki is born
Olaus joins The Wilderness Society	1937	
Olaus completes Jackson Hole elk study	1940	Wangari Maathai is born
Buys ranch; Olaus Director Wilderness Society	1945	World War II ends
Muries lead Sheenjek Expedition in Alaska	1956	Alaska becomes 49th state
	1960	Arctic Nat'l Wildlife Refuge (ANWR)
Olaus dies October 21	1963	
Attends signing of Wilderness Act	1964	Wilderness Act is passed
	1969	Man lands on the moon
	1973	Endangered Species Act is passed
Is appointed to Alaskan task force	1975	
	1980	ANWR gains wilderness protection
Receives the Pres. Medal of Freedom	1998	
Dies October 19	2003	

David Suzuki

1936 – present

Environmental Activist

*"Being an environmental activist means
working for a brighter, cleaner future."*

Both happiness and tragedy marked David's early life. His happiest times were spent fishing and camping with his dad. At the age of four, David took his first fishing trip. Sitting in a boat on the edge of a lake, he carefully lowered his hook and line into the water. When he pulled it up, there was a trout. Again and again he dropped his line. Again and again he pulled up a fish—fifteen in all. His father had picked out a special fishing spot where David was sure to be successful. He knew that if David had fun the first time he tried fishing, he would want to do it again. And David did! Fishing became his lifelong passion.

David and his dad explored many lakes and rivers near their home in British Columbia, Canada. On one trip, it was so hot that his dad told him to jump into the river to cool off. "You mean with my clothes and shoes on?" David asked in disbelief. "Sure," his dad replied.[1] So in he splashed!

On another trip, David and his dad hiked at night to a camping spot. As they made their way through the forest, their dog began to growl. Then they saw two glistening eyes shining in the beam of the flashlight. A bear! David's father stayed calm. Slowly, the bear turned and walked away. David recalled, "Seeing the bear was a fascinating and exciting experience." His father taught him to love and respect nature, but never to fear it.[2]

Tragedy arrived on December 7, 1941—the day Japan bombed Pearl Harbor. Immediately David and his family became "the enemy." Although David and his parents were all born in Canada, his grandparents were from Japan. As a child, David never thought of himself as different from his neighbors. But he was. He looked Japanese, and his name was Japanese.

The Canadian government rounded up everyone of Japanese ancestry on the west coast. Twenty-two thousand Japanese Canadians were forced to leave their homes and businesses, including David and his family. Their rights as Canadian citizens were ignored. David's father was sent to a labor camp, where he worked to build the highway that stretches across Canada. David, his two sisters, and his mother were sent to an internment camp located in an abandoned ghost town. An old hotel became their new "home." It was falling apart and filthy with dirt and bedbugs. Many of the windows didn't have any glass. Food and other supplies were scarce.

David lived in forced isolation and poverty for three years—years that shaped his view of life. He grew up believing that something was wrong with him, that he wasn't worthy. He felt that he constantly had to prove to himself and others that he was good enough. His early experiences in school added to his pain. Bullies picked on him and called him names. When the war ended, his family, like other Japanese-Canadian families, was relocated east of the Rocky Mountains, far from their home in British Columbia. The Suzukis were sent to Ontario. David continued to feel different from his classmates. Not only was he Asian, he was poor. He was embarrassed by his family's old 1929 car and partly-finished house. By the time he got to high school, he was shy and lonely.

Even though he wasn't popular, he was an excellent student. He loved learning, studied hard, and got good grades. After school he would retreat to a large swamp that was a ten-minute bike ride from his house. The natural wonders of the wetland fascinated him, especially the insects. With all of his clothes on, he waded into the water up to his eyeballs, a jar for catching insects in one hand and a net in the other.

During his last year in high school, one of his fellow "outcasts" asked him to run for school president. David thought it was a crazy idea.

David decorated his dad's Model A to campaign for student president in 1953.

He was sure he'd lose. But his father reprimanded him saying, "Whatever you do, there will always be people better than you, but that doesn't mean you shouldn't try. There's no shame in not coming in first."[3] David listened to his father and entered the race. He campaigned as an "Outie"—someone who wasn't part of the popular group of athletes and cheerleaders (the "Innies"). To David's amazement, he won! Little did he know that 41 years later the Canadian people would vote him to be one of the top five Greatest Canadians.

David's good grades earned him a scholarship to an American school: Amherst College in Massachusetts. He had planned to become a doctor, but during his junior year he was required to take a course that changed his life. It was a course in genetics—the study of heredity. David's mother couldn't understand why he would give up a career as a doctor to study fruit flies. (Fruit flies are commonly used for genetic experiments because they reproduce so quickly.) But David knew it was the right decision for him.

After earning a Ph.D. from the University of Chicago, he returned to Canada. In 1963, David became a professor of zoology at the University of British Columbia and set up a research lab. He put all of his energy into working with his students in the lab. It was his favorite place to be. In his autobiography he wrote:

> Evenings were the best time to be in the lab. No one, including me, had classes then, so we could count fruit flies, drink coffee, and talk... The students I attracted were enthusiastic, and the lab became a kind of family. We worked hard, but we also played hard, going to the pub, skateboarding in the basement, camping together on the weekends and in the summers.[4]

A major turning point in his life happened when David read Rachael Carson's book *Silent Spring*. Carson warned about the dangers of using pesticides such as DDT. She explained how they damaged the fragile ecosystem. For David, this was a call to action. Working in his genetics lab, he found a way to control pests without chemicals. He created fruit flies that died in hot weather. By releasing them into the wild, they would mate with regular flies and their offspring would also die in the heat. If insect pests were altered in this way, chemical pesticides would no longer be needed. Natural pest control was a major discovery. From 1969 to 1972, David was named the "Outstanding Research Scientist in Canada Under the Age of 35."

About this same time, David started to gain a reputation as a good speaker. When he was in high school his father had encouraged him to learn how speak in public, so David was comfortable in front of an audience. As a professor, he improved his speaking skills by entertaining his students with interesting lectures. Occasionally he would appear as a guest on science television shows. Then in 1971, he hosted a national TV

David had many different animals on his television program The Nature of Things with David Suzuki.

program called *Suzuki on Science*. He really enjoyed it! So did the viewers. It was on the air for three years.

David believed that through television he could teach the latest scientific developments to lots of people. He also hoped he could influence governments and corporations to give more money to support scientific research. Taking a leave of absence from his job at the university in 1974, he went to work in media. He hosted a TV program, *Science Magazine*, and also a radio program, *Quirks and Quarks*. His unique style and amusing approach to science made both shows very popular.

For over 30 years he has hosted *The Nature of Things with David Suzuki*. It has been one of Canadian television's most popular shows, seen in over 50 countries around the world. The program has led David into many unusual, sometimes dangerous, and often funny situations. He describes some of them in his autobiography.[5] For one show, David had to stand on the wing of an airplane. In case he fell off, he was given a parachute:

> I had never jumped from a plane. Somehow, a one-minute instruction that ended with "If you slip off, just pull this cord and you should be fine" was not that reassuring.

While filming in the Arctic, David had to walk alone onto the ice while a helicopter hovered high overhead:

> At the insistence of our Inuit guides, I had carried a rifle because polar bears are virtually invisible on the ice. They can jump up and attack so quickly and powerfully that I wouldn't have been able to get help before I was killed...That shoot is the only one where I felt the hair stand up on the back of my neck.

For a program about man's relationship with chimpanzees:
> As we began to shoot and I started talking, the chimp reached into the frame and tickled me under the chin! It was a probe of curiosity that

Earth Heroes: Champions of the Wilderness

we could never have rehearsed or trained the animal to perform, and it worked as a perfect surprise for the piece—but I blew it. I was so shocked at the chimp's initiative that I stuttered and then broke out laughing.

Today, David continues to make science understandable, entertaining, and interesting for millions of people. In his opinion, science is the greatest factor shaping our world. The way it is applied to industry, medicine, and the military affects everyone. Many of his shows focus on preserving the wilderness, ecosystems, and wildlife. David strongly believes people can't make the right decisions about important environmental issues, such as climate change and alternative energy, unless they understand scientific concepts.

When he was younger, he never dreamed he would become a television celebrity. But he is. He has become an international spokesperson for science and the environment. He takes this responsibility very seriously. He says, "Regular viewers of *The Nature of Things with David Suzuki* watch the program on faith that what we present is important and true, and they come to expect me to tell them what to do or to act on their behalf."[6]

In addition to his environmental concerns, David has a deep appreciation for native people all around the world. Because of his experience in an internment camp, he has a special understanding of all those who have been driven out of their original homelands. Many of these people look to David for help with their problems.

In 1982, David did a program that focused on the Haida First Nations people. They were fighting to save their ancient forests on the Queen Charlotte Islands along the coast of British Columbia. These rugged islands have been home to the Haida for thousands of years. They used the trees to build their dugout canoes, longhouses, and totem poles.

David began his program by showing viewers the islands' natural beauty. Many of the trees were already mature long before Christopher Columbus discovered America. The TV cameras then scanned huge areas that had been logged. The damage was devastating. In places where the giant trees were clearcut, the topsoil was washed away. The animals lost their habitat. The entire ecosystem was disrupted. David said that the forest would never look the same again.

The program had a huge impact on the people of Canada. Many people wanted to protect the wilderness. However, the logging companies fought hard to resist any restrictions to their cutting. The debate dragged on for years. Finally, in 1987, the government put a stop to the clear cutting. The ancient forests were saved! A six hundred-square-mile area was protected as the Gwaii Haanas National Park Reserve. The park's name means "The Place of Wonder."

The Nlaka'pamux First Nations people also called on David. In 1984, their home in the Stein Valley of southwestern British Columbia was being threatened by logging. The Nlaka'pamux had roamed throughout the valley for thousands of years. It was important to them spiritually, and they used it as a sacred burial site. They also relied on it for food, such as berries and fish.

The First Nations people thought the best way to save the valley was to let others know how special it was. They wanted people to see the valley's spectacular beauty and experience the native culture. David and his wife, Tara, helped them organize a festival. The festival became an annual event. It was attended by thousands of people who wanted the Stein Valley from protected from logging. The government listened to them, and the area is now preserved as a wilderness area.

Getting to know the First Nations people changed David's outlook on life. They told him that all people are made of the four sacred elements: earth, air, fire, and water. As he reflected on that, he realized that he had been thinking about environmental problems in the wrong way. He said: "There's no environment 'out there' for us to interact with. We are the environment because we are the earth. For me, that began a whole shift in the way that I looked at the issues that confront us and the way we live on this planet."[7]

The Kaiapo Indians are another native group David helped. They live in the dense Amazon rain forest in Brazil. David visited them while filming a program about their complex ecosystem. He was saddened to see huge areas of forest cut and burned. The smoke was so thick it was too dangerous for the film crew to fly over the forest. But the Kaiapo depended on the forest. Their culture was being destroyed.

While in the Amazon, David met an extraordinary Kaiapo leader. His name is Paiakan. At the age of seventeen, Paiakan knew he had to help his people. He wanted to learn enough so that he could protect their traditional way of life. He left his remote village and traveled to a Catholic missionary school. After he learned to read and write, he wrote a book about the rain forest as his home. He helped his people by leading them to a brand new village away from any roads. He also took over a gold

Paiakan (top right) lifts an electric eel out of a river in Brazil. David (top left) watches.

mine that was polluting their river. Paiakan spoke out against the destruction of the rain forest, even though he received death threats.

In 1988, Paiakan fought to stop the building of several dams on the Xingu River. The dams would flood nearly 20 million acres of rain forest. Most of the land belonged to the Kaiapo Indians. David and Tara brought Paiakan to Canada to speak to large groups about the destruction the dams would cause. People loved him.

Several newspapers featured colorful photos of Paiakan wearing his headdress of red and blue feathers. He was a clever speaker. When a reporter asked him why he wore paint and feathers, Paiakan responded with his own question, "Why do you wear a tie?"[8]

David, Tara, and Paiakan traveled all over Canada. Everywhere they went, Paiakan pleaded for help in saving the rain forest. In six weeks, they raised thousands of dollars. He used the money to publicize the terrible effects the dams would have on the environment and the people. The dams were never built. Paiakan became a global hero. In 1990, the United Nations Environment Programme listed him as one of the top 500 environmentalists in the world.

Paiakan knew that his people's future depended on keeping the rain forest free from the destruction that comes with development. He wondered how he could convince people that forests are most valuable when left standing. Then he had an idea. He would establish a research station in a remote part of the forest. Scientists could come to learn the forest secrets from the Kaiapo. In turn, the Kaiapo could learn from the scientists.

David thought it was a great idea! To help pay for it, he and Tara organized tours of the Amazon. People were taken into the rain forest to see its amazing plants and animals and experience life in a traditional Indian community. The tours were a huge success. The research station, Project Pinkaiti, was established and is still in operation. Scientists and college students from all over the world come to study there. One of the students was David's daughter, Severn, who did research there in 2001.

The research station is a wonderful example of combining the knowledge of native people with modern science. In his book, *Wisdom of Elders: Sacred Native Stories of Nature*, David wrote that we need the perspectives of both the scientific view of nature and native "ways of knowing." He describes an Aboriginal woman he met in Australia. She took him on a walk around the famous Ayers Rock. At first David saw only sand and scrub. But the woman knew how to find food everywhere. He was amazed as she pointed out tiny edible fruits and various nutritional and medicinal plants.

He believes that modern man has a lot to learn from these people about being connected to nature. In 1989, he learned his own personal lesson about differences in native and modern cultures when he and Tara visited a Kaiapo village. When it was time for them to go, they left a small plastic bag of garbage in their hut. David assumed the Kaiapo would bury it. But when he returned to the same hut ten years later, he was shocked to find the same plastic bag sitting in the corner where he had left it! He came to realize that the Kaiapo live in a world that is totally biodegradable. Everything they use can just be left where it is to decompose.

David developed a greater understanding about the connectedness of all life. He wanted to express his feelings at the Earth Summit in Rio de Janeiro, Brazil. With the help of native friends, he wrote a *Declaration of Interdependence*. It begins:

> We are the earth, through the plants and animals that nourish us.
> We are the rains and the oceans that flow through our veins.
> We are the breath of the forests of the land and the plants of the sea.
> We are human animals, related to all other life as descendants of the
>   firstborn cell.

We share a common present, filled with uncertainty.
We share a common future as yet untold.[9]

Throughout the years, David has alerted people to environmental problems. Many have asked him, "What can I do?" David wanted to give them some answers, but he didn't know the solutions. In 1990, he decided to find them. He formed the David Suzuki Foundation. It is a science-based organization that looks for ways to help people live in balance with the natural world. The foundation states "solutions are in our nature." It focuses on climate change, clean energy, oceans, and sustainability.

The Suzuki Foundation's web site shares up-to-date research on all of these topics. It also has fun and practical projects like growing an organic garden, tips from the "queen of green," and contests for the best nature photos.

David has worked for over fifty years to make a difference in the world. He's been a scientist and a celebrity. As an author, he's written over 43 books (15 for children) and received numerous honors and awards. Because of his work, many places in the environment have been protected and preserved. Even with all of these accomplishments, David says, "Being a parent is the most important thing I have done in life."[10] Two of his daughters, Severn and Sarika, are following in their father's footsteps to protect the environment.

Severn started when she was only nine years old. She founded the Environmental Children's Organization. At age twelve, she attended the Rio Earth Summit. The delegation was stunned by what she said. These are some of her memorable words:

> I am here to speak for the generation to come. . . . I'm only a child, yet I know we are part of a family, five billion strong, in fact, 30 million species strong; and borders and governments will never change that. I am only a child, yet I know we are all in this together and should act as one single world toward one single goal.[11]

She received a standing ovation. Vice-President Al Gore told her, "That was the best speech anyone has given here."[12] The text of her speech is in her book, *Tell the World*. The book also gives teenagers suggestions about what they can do to help the environment. A video of her talk is available on the Internet. Severn continues to speak around the world. As an adult, she is pursuing her passion in ethnobotany, the study of how native people use plants.

Twelve-year-old Severn, David's daughter, delivered a speech at the Earth Summit in Rio de Janeiro in 1992.

Sarika, David's youngest daughter, grew up hearing her father talk about environmental disasters. As a preteen, she began to think that the problems were just too big to solve. David wanted to show her that there were solutions to every problem. He wanted to give her hope for the future.

In 2008, when Sarika was twenty five, David took her to Europe to see solutions that were already working. They documented their journey in a special series for *The Nature of Things* called *The Suzuki Diaries*. While visiting Denmark, she and her dad rode bikes, just like 500,000 Danes do every day. That saves a lot of oil! When they traveled to Berlin, they discovered that Germany is leading the world in alternative energy. In Spain, one of the sunniest countries in the world, they saw how mirrors could be used to concentrate sunlight to use for energy. The *Suzuki Diaries* give a positive look at the future if humans are willing to change how they use energy.

David Suzuki reminds people that all life on Earth is interconnected. He carries this vision into the future as he works for solutions, opportunities, and hope.

FAST FACTS

Born: March 24, 1936, Vancouver, British Columbia, Canada

Wife: Tara Cullis

Children: Tamiko, Troy, Laura, Severn, and Sarika

ACCOMPLISHMENTS:
- Author of 43 books (15 for children)
- Voted one of the top five Greatest Canadians
- Hosted several influential television programs and specials, including *The Nature of Things with David Suzuki*, which has run since 1979
- Champion of the Order of Canada
- Received 20 honorary doctorates from universities in Canada, the U.S., and Australia
- Received six native names and adopted by two tribes.
- Full Professor at University of British Columbia
- Founder of the David Suzuki Foundation

RIPPLES OF INFLUENCE

Famous People Who Influenced David Suzuki
Rachel Carson, E.O. Wilson, Jane Goodall, Richard Leakey, James Lovelock, Al Gore, David Quammen, Carl Safina, Ronald Wright, Bill McKibben, Paiakan. In addition, David Suzuki has been influenced by native people from around the world. He says that the *most* influential person in his life has been his father.

Famous People Influenced by David Suzuki
The Dalai Lama, John Denver, Gordon Lightfoot, Helen Caldicott, David Helvarg, Bill McKibben, Robyn Williams, Richard Mabey

TIMELINE

David Suzuki's Life | Historical Context

David Suzuki's Life		Historical Context
Born March 24	1936	
	1940	Wangari Maathai born
	1941	Japan bombs Pearl Harbor
Put into an internment camp	1942	
Moves to Ontario	1945	
	1948	Aldo Leopold dies
Wins school election	1950	
Graduates, Amherst Col.; marries (1st)	1958	
Earns a Ph.D. in Zoology, Univ. of Chicago	1961	
	1962	Rachel Carson writes *Silent Spring*
	1963	Pres. Kennedy is assassinated
Prof. in genetics dept. at Univ. of B.C.	1963-2001	
	1969	Man lands on the moon
Named Greatest Canadian Scientist under 35	1969-1972	
Hosts *Suzuki on Science, Quirks & Quarks*	1971	
Marries Tara Cullis (2nd marriage)	1972	
	1973	Endangered Species Act becomes law
Becomes an Officer to the Order of Canada	1976	
	1977	Green Belt Movement begins
Host for *The Nature of Things*	1979-pres.	
	1980	Aldo Leopold Wilderness is designated
Airs a show about Haida Gwaii	1982	St. Barbe Baker dies
Helps Nlaka'pamux in Stein Valley	1984	
Receives a United Nations prize for science	1986	
	1987	Logging stops on Haida Gwaii
Meets Paiakan in the Amazon	1988	
Formed the David Suzuki Foundation	1990	
	1991	Japan is world's largest auto maker
Attends Earth Summit in Brazil	1992	
Voted one of the top five Greatest Canadians	2004	
Named Companion to the Order of Canada	2006	
Hosts *The Suzuki Diaries*	2008	First African-American elected Pres. of U.S.

David Suzuki

119

Earth Heroes: Champions of the Wilderness

Wangari Maathai
1940–present

Tree Mother of Africa

"When we plant trees, we plant the seeds of peace and seeds of hope."

How could a poor girl from a remote African village grow up to be a world-famous environmental leader? The answer lies in this story, which Wangari Maathai tells to audiences all over the world.

One day a huge fire broke out in the forest. All of the animals, seeing the flames coming closer and closer, decided to save themselves. They rushed to the edge of the forest, feeling overwhelmed and helpless as they watched the fire spread throughout their forest home.

That is, all animals except one: a hummingbird, who said, "I'm going to do something about the fire!" She flew to the nearest stream, scooped up a drop of water in her beak, and deposited it on the blazing fire. Tirelessly, she flew back and forth from the stream to the fire. Each time she carried a single drop of water and let it fall on the flames.

The other animals watched her with disbelief. "Your are too small," they said. "You cannot hope to put out the fire. What do you think you're doing?"

The little hummingbird scooped up another drop of water and said, "I'm doing the best I can."

For most of her life Wangari has been just like the hummingbird—bit by bit she has done her best in many dangerous and discouraging situations. In 2004 her work was recognized. She received one of the world's highest awards—the Nobel Peace Prize. Wangari made history as the first African woman to receive the prize. She was also the first environmentalist to receive the famous award for promoting world peace. What is the connection between world peace and a healthy environment? The Nobel Committee put it this way: "Peace on earth depends on our ability to secure our living environment."[1]

When Wangari was a child, no one would have guessed the attention of the whole world would focus on her some day. She was born in 1940 in a village in Kenya, Africa. As a little girl she lived on a British settler's farm in the Rift Valley where her parents worked. Her mud-walled, thatch-roofed house didn't have any running water or electricity. She slept on a bed made from wooden planks topped with a mattress stuffed with leaves, ferns, and grass.

The house was small, but it never felt crowded to Wangari because everyone was outside all day long. Every morning Wangari went into the fields with her mother and younger sisters. She played in the soil while her mother planted, weeded, and harvested crops. Fields of maize and wheat stretched as far as she could see. She delighted in watching "waves" ripple through the wheat fields when the wind blew.

When she was seven, Wangari moved to a village in the central highlands where her older brothers were going to school. The sixty-mile trip took all day. As the bus slowly made its way out of the valley that surrounded the farm, Wangari's perspective of the world dramatically changed. She had thought the world ended at the top of the mountain ridges—where the sky and clouds touched the land. But as the bus left the valley, the boundaries of her world expanded. Later she wrote:

> For the first time I came to the top of the ridge, and I discovered that there was something beyond. I was so happy to know that the whole world was not in that valley, that there was another world. That little journey reminds me of the many journeys I have made since. Before

you go, you think the world is just here, and then you go to the ridge and you see there is another world.

There are so many ridges in life, and if you are willing to go to the top, you will see another world beyond. But if you don't go—if you don't take the risk—if you only stay where you're safe, then of course you never see past the ridge.[2]

Following the traditions of her Kikuyu tribe, Wangari was constantly by her mother's side doing everything exactly as her mother did. Gathering firewood for cooking was a frequent activity. Young Wangari often went into the nearby woodlot to gather sticks and carry them home in a bundle on her back. She had her own 15-foot square plot of land in the middle of her mother's field. She planted sweet potatoes, beans, maize, and millet. Wangari sometimes grew impatient waiting for the seeds to germinate, so she would lift them out of the ground to see how quickly they were growing. Her mother cautioned her not to remove the seeds, but to keep them covered. She said, "You have to let them do all this by

Kenyan women carry firewood as Wangari did as a child.

themselves. Soon they will all come above the ground.”[3] And to Wangari's amazement, they did!

Even when she was older and went away to boarding school, she kept her plot of land cultivated. Her mother tended her plants while she was gone. Wangari eagerly anticipated the holidays when she would return home to touch the soil and work in the fields. She thought nothing was more beautiful than cultivating the land at dusk.

> At that time of day in the central highlands, the air and the soil are cool, the sun is going down, the sunlight is golden against the ridges and the green of trees, and there is usually a breeze. As you remove the weeds and press the earth around the crops, you feel content. . . . Earth and water, air and the waning fire of the sun combine to form the essential elements of life and reveal to me my kinship with the soil.”[4]

Sometimes she would get so absorbed in her work that she wouldn't notice that it was getting dark. When she could no longer tell the difference between the weeds she was cutting and the crops she was growing, she would reluctantly walk home.

One of her favorite places to go was a wild fig tree, a tree that was considered sacred by Wangari's tribe. No one took any of its branches or cut the dense undergrowth that grew beneath it. Hundreds of birds would fill the tree's giant canopy when the figs were ripe.

Near the fig tree, water bubbled up out of the ground to form a little stream. Its fresh, cool water was delicious to drink. Arrowroot plants grew all along its banks. Their large, deep green, arching leaves created the perfect hideaway for Wangari. She would sit there for hours, lost in a fascinating natural world.

She especially loved to play with the frogs' eggs she found floating at the water's edge. She thought they looked like sparkling black, brown, and white beads that would make a beautiful necklace. But no matter how carefully she tried to put them around her neck, the jelly that held them together always broke and the little eggs would slip through her fingers. She was so disappointed! Sometimes, instead of eggs, she found tadpoles wriggling in the water. Other times she found frogs hopping around. She never made the connection between the eggs, tadpoles, and frogs until she went to school and learned about the life cycle of amphibians.

In school Wangari also learned about the connection between the fig tree and the stream. "The fig tree's roots burrowed deep into the grouped, breaking through the rocks beneath the surface soil and diving into the underground water table. The water traveled up along the roots until it hit a depression or weak place in the ground and gushed out as a spring."[5] Wherever there were fig trees, there were usually streams nearby.

Most of the girls in Wangari's village didn't get an education. But Wangari's mother decided that she should go to the local missionary school where her brothers went. Because her tribe passed on knowledge through storytelling, Wangari didn't know anything about reading and writing or pencils with erasers. She was truly impressed when she saw her older cousin make marks (letters) across the page of his notebook. But what really fascinated her was when he made the marks disappear by rubbing them with an eraser. It was like magic! From that moment Wangari was motivated to read, write, and rub.

When Wangari was eleven, her mother once again made a momentous decision. She sent Wangari to St. Cecelia's Catholic boarding school. At first Wangari was a little homesick, but she soon adjusted to a happy routine of classes, sports, studying, and church services. The nuns who ran the school were like mothers to her. They were nurturing, encouraging, and compassionate. Wangari often wondered why they would make sacrifices in their own lives to help strangers in a remote part of the world. She was deeply inspired by their service. Wangari carried that inspiration into her adult life.

Wangari's interest in science began in high school.

Her education continued when she went to the only Catholic high school for African girls in Kenya. It was the very first time Wangari was with girls from different regions. It was also the first time she had a pair of shoes. Her science teacher, Mother Teresia, paid special attention to Wangari and invited her into the lab after class. As they washed Petri dishes and test tubes, they would talk. These conversations awakened and encouraged Wangari's lifelong interest in science. Reflecting on her high school experience, Wangari wrote: "After my education by the nuns,

I emerged as a person who believed that society is inherently good and that people generally act for the best."[6]

When Wangari graduated in 1959, she was among a very small number of girls in Kenya who had completed high school. Her options were extremely limited. Going to college was unthinkable to everyone but Wangari. She wanted to continue her studies but didn't know how she would do it. Surprisingly, her opportunity came from the United States.

The U.S. wanted to support Kenya in achieving independence from British rule. Many people in the U.S. realized that Kenya would need to educate their young people to become good leaders. In 1960, John F. Kennedy helped arrange scholarships for over 600 Kenyans to attend American colleges and universities. He also provided the money to fly them to the U.S. for free. This program became known as the "Kennedy Airlift," and Wangari was one of the first students.

To Wangari, landing in New York City in 1960 was like landing on the moon. She had never imagined such a place. It was a "magic city." Her first ride on an escalator was an experience she never forgot. It looked like a snake as it "slithered" between floors.

New York was just a quick stopping point for Wangari. Her final destination was Mount St. Scholastica College in Atchison, Kansas. Like her other schools, it was Catholic. She majored in biology and studied hard to do well. After completing her bachelor's degree, she received a scholarship to the University of Pittsburg where she earned a master's degree in biology.

When she graduated, she was promised a teaching position in Kenya at the University College of Nairobi (later called Nairobi University). Wangari knew she was very privileged to have received five and a half years of excellent education, and she couldn't wait to share her knowledge with others. She was ready to "work hard, help the poor, and watch out for the weak and vulnerable."[7]

Kenya was a free and independent country when Wangari returned home. However, not everyone was treated fairly and equally. Wangari experienced unfair treatment when she showed up for her first day of work at the university. Her job had been given to a man of a different ethnic group. She was shocked and deeply disappointed to discover she was discriminated against. For many months she didn't know what to do.

With the help of some friends, she got a job at the same university in the Department of Veterinary Anatomy. It turned out to be the perfect place for her. Her career there lasted for sixteen years. During that time she helped women break through many of the barriers they faced. She accomplished many "firsts." She became the *first* East and Central African woman to earn a Ph.D.; the *first* woman to become a senior lecturer in anatomy at the university; the *first* woman to become the Department Chair in Veterinary Anatomy; and the *first* woman to become an associate professor.

She discovered that women teaching at the university didn't receive the same salary or benefits as men. Refusing to keep quiet about such an unfair practice, she worked hard to change things. No woman had ever spoken out against the authority of the university! However, that didn't stop her. Eventually the university agreed to pay her the same as the male professors.

Her struggle for equality taught Wangari an important lesson. She had to hold on to what she believed in, even when others opposed her. She would remember this lesson later, when she fought to improve the environment.

In addition to working full-time, Wangari was a wife and a mother of three children. She also strongly believed in serving her country and volunteered in many community organizations. Wangari tried to help women from rural areas. They were living in places just like the village where she had grown up. They told her that they didn't have enough wood for fuel, water to drink, or food for their families and livestock. As Wangari listened, she realized that everything they lacked—energy, water, and food—depended on the environment.

128   Earth Heroes: Champions of the Wilderness

Women of the Green Belt Movement grow seedlings.

She also realized that the environment had drastically changed since she was a child. Native trees had been cut down and replaced with tea and coffee—crops that could be sold for cash. Without the trees, soil was washed into the streams and rivers, making the water too dirty to drink. The number of landslides increased during the rainy season because there were no longer tree roots holding the soil in place. The soil that wasn't washed away was too poor to grow nutritious food. Entire forest ecosystems had been destroyed. The clean water, fertile soil, and the tadpoles that Wangari had loved as a child were gone.

As a result of her education in America, Wangari had learned to look for solutions to problems. And she didn't want to just *talk* about solutions. She wanted to take action! She believed the solution to the women's problems was to plant trees.

Trees would help women in so many ways. They would give shade and prevent the soil from being washed away. As the trees grew, they would provide firewood, building materials, and fruit. Trees would allow the rainwater to seep slowly into the ground to refill the underground reservoirs, instead of rushing down the barren hillsides washing away the soil.

Planting trees was not a new idea for Wangari. She had always loved trees. She remembered the fig tree from her childhood and how her father planted trees on the farm in the Rift Valley. In 1975, she had tried to get Kenyans interested in planting trees as a business. Although the business didn't succeed, she held on to the idea.

She knew that Kenyans had a history of planting trees. They had helped St. Barbe Baker begin the international tree-planting organization, the Men of the Trees, in the 1920s. Wangari used the Kenyan word *harambee* to describe the spirit of her tree-planting campaign. *Harambee* means "let us all pull together."

Wangari and a group of women began by planting seven trees in a Nairobi park in 1977. Since that day her small group has grown into an international organization called the Green Belt Movement. They have planted over 30 million trees in 12 African countries. These trees have restored the health of many local ecosystems. And just as important, the Green Belt Movement has helped rural African people become good custodians of their local environment. As Wangari writes in *The Green Belt Movement*, they "do what is right for the environment because their hearts have been touched and minds convinced."[8]

When it first started, the Green Belt Movement had to overcome many obstacles. One problem was not having enough tree seedlings to plant. Wangari's solution was to have the women grow their own seedlings in tree nurseries. The official Kenyan foresters didn't think the rural women had enough training to manage nurseries. Wangari disagreed. She knew the women already grew many kinds of plants from seed. She

"Foresters without diplomas" work at a tree nursery in Tumutumu Hills, Kenya. The Green Belt Movement planted over 30 million trees in 12 African countries.

130 Earth Heroes: Champions of the Wilderness

thought they just had to treat the tree seeds as they would any other seeds—make a hole, plant the seed, and water it. She advised them, "Just use your woman sense."[9] They were incredibly resourceful as they taught each other the most successful ways to plant and grow trees. Wangari called them "foresters without diplomas."

Other obstacles were more challenging and complicated. Kenya's environmental problems were connected to its social problems, economy, and politics. There were many injustices in Kenya, and Wangari spoke out against all of them. She opposed the government when it tried to sell public forestlands to private investors who wanted to cut down all the trees. She supported democracy and the rights of women and children. She protested the imprisonment of political dissidents who weren't given a trial. The government saw her as its enemy, and Wangari was regularly arrested and thrown into jail without food or water. During one demonstration, she was beaten unconscious by the police.

Such hardships would have caused many people to give up. But despite all of her challenges, Wangari's philosophy of life kept her going strong. She believes every experience has a lesson to teach. Every situation has a silver lining. Wangari's mother was one the most important influences in her life. Her mother's contentment and composure inspired Wangari. Now Wangari inspires others by showing them how to stay focused on what they want to attain. She reminds them to resist their fears and just keep moving forward.

No matter how much pressure the government applied on Wangari, she and the members of the Green Belt Movement continued to plant trees. People would sometimes ask her why an educated person like herself would dig in the soil on her hands and knees. She should leave such work to others, they said. She would reply that education shouldn't take people away from the land. It should help them have more respect for it because they can understand what will be lost if the environment isn't protected. She said, "All species need to be protected, not just because we love them, but because we *need* them." [10]

Wangari Maathai

To explain the connection she saw between the environment and government, she compared a country to an African stool with three legs and a seat on top. One leg of the stool is democracy and human rights. Another leg is a healthy environment and good management of natural resources. The third leg is an atmosphere of peace so that people feel safe. The top of the stool, the seat, is the country. If all three legs are in place, the country is strong and stable. It can grow and develop. Without all three legs the country will fall.

Wangari wanted to help her country become a strong democracy that used its resources wisely. She ran for a seat in Kenya's Parliament in 2002 and won with a 98% majority of the votes. She is now working to make sure that Kenya has all three legs of its stool in place.

Wangari's receiving the Nobel Peace Prize helped the world recognize the important connections between peace and the environment, human rights, and democracy. On the day she won the prize, Wangari planted a tree. Trees give her hope. She said:

> What I have learned over the years is that we must be patient, persistent, and committed. When we are planting trees sometimes people will say to me, 'I don't want to plant this tree because it will not grow fast enough.' I have to keep reminding them that the trees they are cutting today were not planted by them, but by those who came before. So they must plant the trees that will benefit communities in the future.[11]

Since winning the Nobel Peace Prize, Wangari has focused on the issue of deforestation and global warming. She was surprised to learn that 20% of the greenhouse gases in Earth's atmosphere are a result of deforestation—cutting and burning trees. That is more than from cars, planes, and other forms of transportation combined. Protecting existing forests and planting new trees is one of the solutions to the problem of global warming. Forests trap carbon dioxide and provide biodiversity. She wants all countries to understand that their forests are more valuable when they are left standing than when they are cut.

In addition to the Nobel Prize, Wangari has won over 40 national and international awards. One of them was the Digitas Humana Award from St. John's University in Collegeville, Minnesota. She received the award for her work in bringing dignity to the lives of so many people, especially poor women and children.

She told the audience attending the award ceremony about the Japanese concept of *mottainai*. It means being grateful for resources and not wasting them. In the United States a similar concept is the "3 Rs: Reduce, Reuse, and Recycle." Wangari likes to add one more "R" for "Repair."[12] She believes everyone can repair resources where necessary.

Wangari wants the whole world to practice *mottainai*. She practiced it herself when she asked the President of Kenya why the government wasted so much paper. She said, "Books are printed on both sides of the page. Why does our government only use one side of a page?" He considered her question and immediately made it mandatory for all government offices to use both sides of each piece of paper. By questioning what was being done, she made a big difference in the amount of paper that her government uses.

Wangari believes that everyone can do something. She says, "Look around during your daily life. See what needs doing? Ask: how can I help?"[13]

Wangari emphasizes that it's important for young people to prepare themselves for their future role in the world. She tells them to become grounded in good values and learn all that they can so that when they are adults they can contribute to finding solutions to challenges. In her Nobel Prize acceptance speech, Wangari gave a call to action: "I would like to call on young people to commit themselves to activities that contribute toward achieving their long-term dreams. You are a gift to your communities and indeed the world. You are the hope and our future."

FAST FACTS

Born: April 1, 1940, Ihithe, British Kenya

Children: Waweru, Wanjira, and Muta

ACCOMPLISHMENTS:
- Winner of the 2004 Nobel Peace Prize
- Founder and Director of the Green Belt Movement
- First woman to earn a Ph.D. in East and Central Africa
- First woman to hold the following positions at the University of Nairobi: Senior Lecturer in Anatomy, Chair of the Department of Veterinary Anatomy, and Associate Professor of Veterinary Anatomy
- Thirteen honorary degrees
- Over 40 national and international awards
- Author of two books: *Unbowed* and *The Green Belt Movement*

RIPPLES OF INFLUENCE:

Famous People Who Influenced Wangari:
John F. Kennedy, Vice President Al Gore, Richard St. Barbe Baker. She was also greatly influenced by her mother and the Catholic nuns who taught her.

Famous People Influenced by Wangari:
Although Wangari influences many individuals around the world, she works on a large scale influencing change through global organizations such as the United Nations Environmental Programme, The Economic, Social, and Cultural Council of the African Union (ECOSOCC), the Clinton Global Initiative, and National Council of Women of Kenya

TIMELINE

Wangari Maathai's Life		Historical Context
	1880s	Missionaries arrive in Africa
	1890s	British arrive in Kenya
	1922	St. Barbe Baker begins Men of the Trees
	1936	David Suzuki is born
	1939	World War II begins in Europe
Born April 1	1940	
Begins primary school run by missionaries	1947	
	1948	Aldo Leopold dies
	1950s	Mau Mau Rebellion (war of independence)
Boards at St. Cecilia's Intermediate School	1951	
Boards at Loreto-Limuru Girls' High School	1956	
Begins Mt. St. Scholastica College in U.S.	1960	Kennedy Airlift of African students
	1963	Pres. Kennedy assassinated
	1964	Kenya becomes an independent country
Earns masters degree from Univ. Pittsburg	1965	
Begins work at University College of Nairobi	1966	
Marries Mwangi Mathai	1969	
Fights for equal pay; earns Ph.D.	1971	
Becomes Chair of Dept. Veterinary Anatomy	1974	
Begins Green Belt; becomes Assoc. Prof.	1977	
Jailed as a result of divorce proceedings	1979	
Tries to run for Parliament; loses job at univ.	1982	St. Barbe Baker dies
	1982-1992	Kenyan gov't. arrests protestors
	1992	Multi-party elections held in Kenya
Expands GBM to other African countries	1986	
Organizes protests against building in park	1989	
Protests gov't. selling public land	1998	
Elected to Kenyan Parliament	2002	Democratic reforms in Kenya
Asst. Minister for Environment & Nat. Res.	2003-2007	
Receives Nobel Peace Prize	2004	
Taking Root, film about her life, is released	2008	

BECOME A HERO!

RIPPLES OF INFLUENCE

When you throw a pebble into a lake, you can watch the ripples spread out across the water. A tiny pebble can create a very wide circle. Each of these champions sent out a ripple of influence to others in the world. Similarly, each person was influenced by others (in many cases by another Earth Hero). Every ripple increased awareness about wilderness and love for nature.

Henry David Thoreau's writings influenced John Muir.

John Muir's love of nature influenced Teddy Roosevelt

Teddy Roosevelt's policies affected Aldo Leopold's perspective.

Aldo Leopold worked in The Wilderness Society with Mardy and Olaus Murie.

Mardy Murie influenced President Carter.

President Carter signed the Wilderness Act that continues to influence every American.

The ripples keep on spreading outward. By reading this book you've been touched by a ripple. Who will your ripple touch? How will your ripple influence others?

FINDING YOUR WILDERNESS

As you discovered from the stories, the wild places each of the heroes loved were both large (Mardy Murie's Alaska) and small (David Suzuki's swamp). Have you been in a wild place? You may find one as close as your own backyard or neighborhood park. Or maybe it is a special place you visit only once a year (like Aldo Leopold's Marquette Island). Your personal "wilderness" is any place you go to make a connection with nature. As you become familiar with one place in nature, doors will open for you to experience other places, too. Many wild and beautiful places are waiting for you.

OPEN THE DOOR AND GO OUTSIDE

All of the Earth Heroes spent hours outside in nature when they were children. Some watched birds, others planted gardens, and many of them hunted and fished. They experienced the fun of exploring on their own. Their early experiences opened their eyes to nature's mysteries. Start your exploring by doing one the following activities.*

Adventure

- Take a night hike with a flashlight.
- Sleep outside.
- Learn to rock climb.

Animal Allies

- Watch birds. Put up a feeder and birdbath.
- Collect lightning bugs at dusk. Release them at dawn.
- Raise butterflies from caterpillar to chrysalis to emerging butterfly to egg back to caterpillar.

Special Places

- Build a tree house, fort, or hut.
- Set up a backyard weather station. Watch the clouds.
- Find a favorite tree and visit it again and again throughout the year.

Small Wonders

- Keep a terrarium or aquarium.
- Place a piece of scrap wood on bare dirt. Wait two days and lift the board. Count the creatures you find hiding there. Use a field guide to identify them.
- Use a hand lens to observe bugs, leaves, and bark. Crawl under bushes to find what's hiding there.

Search and Find

- Play "Ten Treasures." Go on a walk to find ten different "critters." (mammals, birds, insects, reptiles, snails, other creatures)
- Collect stones, rocks, shells, leaves, or fossils.

Family Fun

- Find an adult nature companion. All of the Earth Heroes had an adult—their father, mother, or grandparent—who encouraged them to explore nature at an early age.

- Establish a "green hour" as a new family tradition. Everyone does an activity outside. It may be as simple as watching the stars come out.

*Special thanks to Richard Louv, *Last Child in the Woods: Saving Our Children from Nature-Deficit Disorder* and David T. Sobel, *Childhood and Nature: Design Principles for Educators* for some of the above ideas.

WALK IN THEIR FOOTSTEPS

Each of the heroes had a place that was special to them. You can go there too. Visit the places listed below to walk where they walked and to see what they saw.

Henry David Thoreau: Sit by Walden Pond and walk through a replica of Henry's cabin. Walden Pond State Reservation, http://www.mass.gov/dcr/parks/walden

John Muir: Experience the mountains, trees, and animals that John loved. Yosemite National Park, http://www.nps.gov/yose

Teddy Roosevelt: Teddy loved the Wild West feeling of the Badlands. Badlands National Park, http://www.nps.gov/badl/index.htm

Aldo Leopold: See the pines that Aldo and his family planted near the "Shack." The Aldo Leopold Foundation, http://www.aldoleopold.org

Richard St. Barbe Baker: Walk through a forest of "wonder trees." Redwood National Park, http://www.nps.gov/redw

Mardy Murie: Visit Mardy's log home and view an elk herd. The Murie Center and U.S. Fish and Wildlife Service, http://www.muriecenter.org/ http://www.fws.gov/refuges/profiles/index.cfm?id=61550

David Suzuki: Hike through the wilderness that David helped preserve in the Stein Valley Nlaka'pamux Provincial Park, http://www.britishcolumbia.com/parks/?id=269

Wangari Maathai: For a really big adventure, travel to Kenya for a Green Belt Safari. The Green Belt Movement, http://www.greenbeltmovement.org/

MAKE A DIFFERENCE

Choose something positive to do for the environment in your own area. As Wangari Maathai says: "No matter who or where we are, or what our capabilities. We are called to do the best we can!"

ABOUT THE AUTHORS AND ILLUSTRATOR

As young children, both Bruce and Carol Malnor were influenced to love nature. Bruce's father and grandparents taught him to explore the woods, lakes, and rivers of Michigan's Upper Peninsula, while Carol discovered natural wonders at National Parks with her family. As educators for over 30 years, that ripple of influence spread to their students. They took their students on many outdoor adventures—hiking, camping, white water rafting, and rock climbing.

Bruce and Carol have conducted educational and environmental workshops in the U.S. and abroad. They have co-authored a series of teacher's guides for Dawn Publications. After several years of writing graduate courses for teachers, Carol now writes for a variety of audiences. Bruce continues to work with teachers as an educational consultant. Their current passions are birding, photography, and enjoying the natural beauty near their home in the foothills of the Sierra Nevada Mountains.

Anisa is a young artist with a fine sense of the human form. Her figures come alive with depth of character and expression. These black and white illustrations are based on careful research. She previously illustrated two full-color picture books, *If You Give a T-Rex a Bone* and *Eliza and the Dragonfly*, which was named Best Picture Book of the Year by the International Reading Association. Anisa is a graduate of the Maryland Institute College of Art. She lives near Seattle on the shores of Lake Washington where she paints, illustrates, and is a massage and cranial-sacral therapist.

ENDNOTES AND PHOTO CREDITS

HENRY DAVID THOREAU

1: Edward Emerson, "Henry Thoreau as Remembered by a Young Friend Edward Emerson, 1917," American Transcendentalism Web <http://www.vcu.edu/engweb/transcendentalism/authors/thoreau/youngfriend.html> (March 2008).

2: Hilda White, *Truth is My Country: Portraits of Eight New England Authors* (New York: Doubleday, 1971).

3: Gordon S. Haight, *Walden: Edited with Notes and Introduction* (Roslyn, NY: Walter J. Black Company).

4: Ralph Waldo Emerson, "Thoreau [Eulogy, 1862]" American Transcendentalism Web <http://www.vcu.edu/engweb/transcendentalism/authors/emerson/essays/thoreau.html> (March 2008).

5, 6, 7: Walter Harding, *The Days of Henry Thoreau: A Biography* (New York: Knopf, 1962).

8: August Derleth, *Concord Rebel: A Life of Henry David Thoreau* (New York: Chilton, 1962).

PHOTO CREDITS: p. 9, Library of Congress; pp. 13 and 14, The Thoreau Institute at Walden Woods; p. 13 (cabin exterior), Martin Schwalbaum, www.4peaks.com; p. 14, Aaron Yates.

JOHN MUIR

1: John Muir, *The Mountains of California* (New York: The Century Company, 1894).

2, 3, 4, 5: *John Muir, The Story of My Boyhood and Youth* (New York: Houghton Mifflin, 1913).

6: *John Muir, My First Summer in the Sierra* (New York: Houghton Mifflin, 1911).

7, 8, 11: Linnie Marsh Wolf, *Son of the Wilderness: The Life of John Muir* (New York: Knopf, 1947).

9: Joseph Cornell, *John Muir: My Life with Nature* (Nevada City, CA: Dawn Publications, 2000).

10: "John Muir Exhibit," Sierra Club <http://www.sierraclub.org/john_muir_exhibit> (February 2008).

PHOTO CREDITS: p. 28, Wisconsin Historical Society, Image ID #10983; pp. 34 and 36, Library of Congress; p. 36, Letter to Janet Moores with self-portrait, 1887, John Muir Papers, Holt-Atherton Special Collections, University of the Pacific Library. Copyright 1984 Muir-Hanna Trust.

THEODORE ROOSEVELT

1: Edward Wagenknecht, *The Seven Worlds of Theodore Roosevelt* (New York: Longmans, Green, and Company, 1958).

2, 8: Kathleen Dalton, *Theodore Roosevelt: A Strenuous Life* (New York: Knopf, 2002).

3, 4: Edmund Morris, *The Rise of Theodore Roosevelt* (New York: The Modern Library, 2001).

5: Betsy Harvey Kraft, *Theodore Roosevelt: Champion of the American Spirit* (New York: Clarion Books, 2003).

6, 7: Paul R. Cutright, *Theodore Roosevelt: The Naturalist* (New York: Harper Collins, 1956).

9: Paul R. Cutright, *Theodore Roosevelt: The Making of a Conservationist* (Urbana: University of Illinois Press, 1985).

10, 11: Brian Manetta, "John Muir, Gifford Pinchot, and the Battle for Hetch Hetchy," Ithaca College <http://www.ithaca.edu/hs/history/journal/papers/sp02muirpinchothetchy.html> (April 2008).

12: Jean Fritz, *Bully for You, Teddy Roosevelt!* (New York: Putnam, 1991).

PHOTO CREDITS: Library of Congress

ALDO LEOPOLD

1, 9, 10: Aldo Leopold, *A Sand County Almanac: With Essays on Conservation from Round River*, (New York: Ballantine, 1970).

2, 3, 4, 5, 6: Curt Meine, *Aldo Leopold: His Life and Work* (Madison, WI: The University of Wisconsin Press, 1988).

7: Steve Nix, "A Leopold Biography: Interview with Marybeth Lorbiecki," About.com: Forestry <http://forestry.about.com/cs/foresthistory1/a/al_leo_lorb1.htm> (June 2008).

8: The Aldo Leopold Foundation <http://www.aldoleopold.org/> (June 2008).

PHOTO CREDITS: The Aldo Leopold Foundation.

RICHARD ST. BARBE BAKER

1, 2, 3, 4, 5, 6, 7, 9, 10, 11, 13, 16: Richard St. Barbe Baker, *My Life, My Trees* (Scotland: The Findhorn Press, 1985).

8, 9: Barrie Oldfield, *Men of the Trees* Western Australia <menofthetrees.com.au> (October 2008).

12: Edward Goldsmith, "The Vision of St. Barbe Baker," *The Ecologist*, July/August 1982.

14: Frank Smith, "A Legend Lives on in the Salty West," *ECOS Magazine*, June/July 2007.

15: "Dr. Richard St. Barbe Baker, O.B.E.," Saskatchewan's Environmental Champions <http://www.econet.sk.ca/sk_enviro_champions/richard_baker.html> (September 2008).

17: Tree People with Andy and Katie Lipkis, *The Simple Act of Planting a Tree* (Los Angeles: Jeremy P. Tarcher, Inc., 1990).

PHOTO CREDITS:

p. 75, iStock photo Frank Leung, www.istock.com; p. 77, Richard St. Barbe Baker, *African Drums*; p. 81, Library of Congress; p. 83, Findhorn Foundation; p. 84, International Tree Foundation.

MARGARET MURIE

1, 4, 7, 8, 22: Charles Craighead and Bonnie Kreps, *Arctic Dance: The Mardy Murie Story* (Portland, OR: Graphic Arts Center Publishing, 2006).

2, 3, 5, 6, 9, Margaret E. Murie, *Two in the Far North* (Seattle, WA: Alaska Northwest Books, 1997).

10, 11, 12: Anne T. Keene, *Earthkeepers: Observers and Protectors of Nature*, (New York: Oxford University Press, 1994).

PHOTO CREDITS: pp. 90, 97, 98, and 102, The Murie Center Archives; p. 95, U.S. Fish and Wildlife Digital Asset Library.

DAVID SUZUKI

1, 2: David Suzuki, *Metamorphosis: Stages in a Life* (Sydney, Australia: Allen & Unwin, 1988).

3, 4, 5, 6, 8, 9, 10, 11: David Suzuki, *David Suzuki: The Autobiography* (Vancouver: Greystone Books, 2006).

7: *Suzuki Speaks*, DVD (Avanti Pictures, 2003).

PHOTO CREDITS: pp. 107, 113, and 117; Dr. Suzuki and Greystone Books, *David Suzuki: The Autobiography*; p. 109, CBC still photo collection; p. 118, Kent Kallberg.

WANGARI MAATHAI

1: Nobel Peace Prize <http://nobelprize.org/nobel_prizes/peace/laureates/2004 (October 2008).

2: My Hero Project, *My Hero: Extraordinary People on the Heroes Who Inspire Them* (New York: Free Press, 2005).

3, 4, 5, 6, 7, 9: Wangari Muta Maathai, *Unbowed: A Memoir*, (New York: Anchor Books, 2007).

8: Wangari Maathai, *The Green Belt Movement: Sharing the Approach and the Experience* (New York: Lantern Books, 2003).

10, 13: Digitas Humana Award Ceremony, St. John's School of Theology and Seminary, Collegeville, MN, October 2008.

11: Curt Schleier, "Growing Trees and Democracy: The Long View," *Investor's Business Daily*, Nov. 7, 2006.

12: Originally suggested by Klaus Töpfer, the head of the UN Environment Programme.

PHOTO CREDITS: p.123, The Green Belt Movement Archives, The Green Belt Movement; p. 129, Ariel Poster, *Taking Root*, Marlborough Productions; p. 130, Alan Dater, *Taking Root*, Marlborough Productions; p. 134, Martin Rowe, The Green Belt Movement.

Endnotes and Photo Credits

INDEX

Agassiz, Louis 28, 36

Alaska 5, 32, 37, 87-89, 92-94, 97-99, 100-103, 136

Alcott, Amos Bronson 11, 15, 20

American Museum of Natural History 40-41

Arctic 88, 99-100, 102-103, 110

Arizona 55, 62, 69

Australia 25, 80, 85, 115, 118

Baker, Richard St. Barbe 69, *70-85*, 103, 119, 129, 134-135, 138

beavers 74

bees 73-74

Bhagavad Gita 12

birds 7, 15, 17, 19, 24, 26-27, 30, 39, 40-44, 46, 48, 50, 52, 56-57, 59, 78, 94-95, 121, 124, 136-137

Boone and Crockett Club 42

botany 28

Brazil 50, 53, 113, 115, 119

Burroughs, John 18, 20, 36, 46, 47, 52

California 21, 23, 30, 35-37, 42, 81-82, 84, 87

Canada 29, 37, 74-75, 84-85, 105-106, 108, 112, 114, 118-119

caribou 93, 96

Carson, Rachael 108, 118-119

Civil Disobedience 18

climate change 20, 111; see also global warming

conservationists 49, 61, 64, 66, 72, 75, 99, 102

Denmark 117

dogs 5, 58, 67, 93-94, 97, 105

ecology 60, 64, 68

Egypt 40-41

elk 43, 46, 98-99, 103, 138

Emerson, Ralph Waldo 10-12, 14-15, 17, 20, 28, 33, 36-37, 58, 68, 84

England 72, 76, 79, 80, 82, 84-85

Fairbanks 87-94, 103

First Nations 74, 111-112

fish, fishing 8, 50, 58, 91-92, 105, 112, 136

Florida 30-31

forestry 60, 62, 64, 76, 80, 82, 84-85

Forest Service 35, 45, 48, 53, 60, 62-63, 66, 69

Gandhi, Mahatma 18, 20

Germany 117

glaciers 4-5, 32, 48

global warming 132-133; see also climate change

Green Belt Movement 119, 129-131, 134-135, 138

Harvard 8, 21, 42, 53

Hetch Hetchy Valley 35, 37, 49, 103

hiking 17, 45-46, 58, 61, 93, 99, 105, 137-139, 144

hunting 8, 41-42, 49, 53, 56-57, 59, 63-64,100

Indiana 29, 31

International Tree Foundation 80

Iowa 56, 58, 68

142   Earth Heroes: Champions of the Wilderness

jail 18, 21, 131, 135

Japan 105-106, 119, 133

Kansas 127

Kenya 76-78, 80, 85, 122-135, 138

Kikuyu tribe 76-78, 123

King, Martin Luther 18, 20

Leopold, Aldo 36-37, 53, *54-69*, 85, 102, 119, 135-136

Maathai, Wangari 5, 69, 78, 84-85, 103, 119, *120-135*, 138

Massachusetts 7, 20, 107

Minnesota 133

Mount Rushmore 50, 51

Muir, John 18, 20-21, *22-37*, 46, 48-49, 52-53, 60-61, 68, 99, 103, 136, 138

Murie, Margaret 5, 37, 53, 69, 85, *86-103*, 136

National Wilderness Preservation System 64, 100

National Wildlife Federation 51, 102

New Jersey 58

New Mexico 62-63, 66, 69, 85

New York 12, 21, 37, 39, 40, 42, 44, 52-53, 127

Nigeria 78, 85

North Dakota 43

Oregon 21, 92

Pinchot, Gifford 35, 48-49, 52, 60-61, 68

preservationist 49, 60-61

rain forest 78-79, 113-114

redwood 48, 81-82, 84-85, 138

Roosevelt, Theodore 5, 21, 34, 36-37, *38-53*, 60, 68-69, 85, 103, 136, 138

Sahara Desert 82, 85

San Francisco 30-31, 35, 37, 49, 53, 69, 85

Scotland 24, 36, 83

Sierra Club 23, 34, 36-37, 100

Sierra Nevada Mountains 30-31, 139

Smithsonian Institution 17, 41, 49

South Dakota 50

Spain 117

Spanish-American War 44

Suzuki, David 5, 69, 85, 103, *104-119*, 135-136,138

Thoreau, Henry David 5, *6-21*, 28, 36-37, 53, 68, 136, 138

Transcendentalist 11-12

trees 7-8, 15, 17-18, 21, 23, 28, 30, 35, 42, 46, 48, 56-57, 64, 66, 71-85, 90, 97, 111-112, 121, 124-125, 129, 130-132, 135, 138

Walden 4-5, 7-8, 12-18, 21, 37, 138

Washington D.C. 41, 46, 48, 94, 97

Wilderness Society 64, 68-69, 99-100, 103, 136

Wildlife Refuge System 45, 99, 101-103

Wisconsin 26, 28-29, 33, 37, 56, 63-64, 68-69

World War I 37, 50, 53, 69, 74, 76, 85

World War II 69, 85, 103, 135

Wyoming 98, 102-103

Yale 60, 69

Yellowstone 42, 46, 48

Yosemite 4, 30, 32-37, 46, 48-49, 138

ALSO IN THE EARTH HEROES SERIES

Earth Heroes: Champions of the Wild Animals features the youth and careers of eight of the world's greatest environmentalists who championed the protection of wildlife. It includes William Hornaday (bison), Ding Darling (ducks), Rachel Carson (birds and other species), Roger Tory Peterson (birds), R.D. Lawrence (wolves), E.O. Wilson (ants), Jane Goodall (chimpanzees), and Iain and Saba Douglas-Hamilton (elephants).

Earth Heroes: Champions of the Ocean portrays environmentalists who loved the ocean and its creatures. Included are William Beebe, Archie Carr, Jacques Cousteau, Margaret Wentworth Owings, "Shark Lady" Eugenie Clark, Roger Payne, Sylvia Earle, and Tierney Thys.

FOR TEACHERS

Lesson Plans for each book in the Earth Heroes series and suggestions for using them are available at www.dawnpub.com under "Activities."

OTHER NOTABLE BOOKS FROM DAWN PUBLICATIONS

Girls Who Looked Under Rocks portrays the youths and careers of six remarkable women whose curiosity about nature fueled a passion to steadfastly overcome obstacles to careers in traditionally men-only occupations. The six—Maria Merian (b.1647), Anna Comstock (b.1854), Frances Hamerstrom (b.1907), Rachel Carson (b.1907), Miriam Rothschild (b.1908), and Jane Goodall (b.1934)—all became renowned scientists, artists and writers. These stories can be a starting point for issues of gender, science, and the environment.

John Muir: My Life with Nature This unique "autobiography" of John Muir is told in his own words, brimming with his spirit and his adventures. The text was selected and retold by naturalist Joseph Cornell, author of Sharing Nature with Children, who is well known for his inspiring nature games.

How We Know What We Know About Our Changing Climate When the weather changes daily, how do we really know that Earth's climate is changing? Here is the science behind the headlines - evidence from flowers, butterflies, birds, frogs, trees, glaciers and much more, gathered by scientists from all over the world. This high-acclaimed book has won 12 awards. A teacher's guide is available.

Dawn Publications is dedicated to inspiring in children a deeper understanding and appreciation for all life on Earth. To review our titles or to order, please visit us at www.dawnpub.com, or call 800-545-7475.